The Bridge at the Place c

Bristol's name can be traced back to the 1050s [I' the bridge. But the term 'bridge' was not clearly de ary defines it, in addition to the usual sense, as stage, jetty or pier'. Bridge End in Lincolnshire's London from at least the 14th century, it defined often stone jetties or quays, with a floating stage arrival of royalty. Many wealthy merchants and city leaders lived in nearby L... shipful Street, which adds weight to this suggestion.

No evidence exists of a bridge over the Avon before the stone bridge was built in the mid 13th century, though claims were made that parts of a wooden bridge were found during the 18th century rebuilding. Adams' Chronicle of 1247 is quite clear on the origins and the reason for its construction: 'And this year the bridge of Bristol began to be founded, the inhabitants of Redcliffe, Temple and Thomas were incorporated and combined with the town of Bristol.'[3]

This fits with the national trend, ie 'Between the 8th and 13th centuries, road travel in England was transformed. There was a shift from a road system focused on fords to be based on a vast network of bridges and causeways.' [4]This period also coincides with the great period of cathedral building. 'Bridges … mirrored the remarkable feats of medieval cathedral builders…This required not only engineering skills but also the ability to work masonry with great precision.'[5]

The medieval bridge was built to unite the southern parishes with the main port, and coincided with the digging of The Old Cut, to divert the Frome and enlarge the quays at a time of a massive influx of money and labour. Likewise, the rebuilding in the mid 18th century was triggered by economic expansion from trade with the American colonies, and increasing population, so the bridge can be seen as an indicator of the city's wealth at the time.

Bristol Bridge was the main crossing between Somerset and Gloucestershire, so formed an important part of the pilgrims' way between Gloucester and Glastonbury. The chapel in the centre housed the city's tallest spire, at 100ft. Dedicated to Our Lady of the Annunciation.

Saxon bridges tended to be built and maintained by locals, but under the Normans, 'the construction and repair of bridges was seen as an important act of charity. New bridges were, like hospitals, schools and almshouses, funded by private bequests, some of which were huge. The link with religion was symbolised by the bridge chapel which was a feature of most major bridges'. [6] William of Worcestre, the tireless pacer- out of his home town, only recorded a single piece of stained glass in the city in 1480 and that was in the bridge chapel, showing local merchants and their wives, probably the original founders. [7]

It is unclear when houses first appeared on it, but 18th Century historian Seyer claims some existed in 1314. The Great Red Book of Bristol for 1376 [8] makes note of a plumber being paid for the maintenance of the Carmelite Conduit (now St John's pipe) from rents of several houses on the bridge at Bristol. Latimer notes[9] 'soon after the Corporation had obtained the Royal Grant of the Chapel on Bristol Bridge, it undertook a work of some importance -the construction of two houses on the same thoroughfare of a character far surpassing the customary style of tradesman's dwellings which rarely exceeded two stories in height' A carpenter was brought from London to superintend the work which began in 1548, at a cost of £495, slightly more than the Council House and Tolzey, rebuilt soon after, so must have been significant. Later records and pictures show they were built on arches hanging over the water, with shops on pavement level and living quarters above. 'Many of the old and affluent citizens lived and made fortunes there. Alderman Stecker founded the hospital on Old Market and kept a grocers' shop there. When Royalist forces came to Bristol, they plundered houses there, allegedly the most disaffected, but more likely because they were the richest' [10]. The future Archbishop of York, Dr Tobias Matthews, was born over his father's shop there [11]. Some historians claim a fire damaged houses there, which is largely refuted by archeologists, but it might explain the lack of historical records.

It was one of the few sites where fresh air could regularly blow away the stench of the city, and tides carried away the sewage and waste. Houses on Old London Bridge were likewise the most desirable, producing total rents of £538 per year, one was even home to a large live camel [12]. When the plague ravaged London, only two of its victims were living on the bridge. The only real inconvenience was the occasional bowsprit of a vessel running through a kitchen window or cattle running through the shops into the river.

Large and famous coaching inns were found in the southern parishes for travellers to Bath and London. Country folk brought produce to market by foot, and farmers drays brought produce to feed the city, returning with dung to fertilise their crops.

But the passage on the bridge was increasingly dangerous. Jeffries [13] noted 'When wheel-carriages were permitted to pass over and increasing prosperity of the country made communicating by carriages increasingly frequent, insufficiency of the bridge became more apparent. At this time shops had encroached on the public way, narrow as it was; for bulks – that is, projecting shelves on which goods were exposed for sale – had been added to the shops, so the way was scarcely sufficient for two carriages to pass and foot passages were forced to shelter in shop doors, many limbs were broken and other accidents; lately when a prospect of the bridge being taken down, many of the houses were untenanted, therefore less places for refuge so further increased accidents.' As early as 1607 Latimer records that a chain was ordered to be placed across the Bridge End to stop vehicles on market days [14].

In June 1758 Felix Farley reported [15] 'a woman coming over the Bridge was met by a cart, and the shaft taking her on the Breast fix't her against one of the shop-posts; she expired immediately on the spot – many limbs and lives have been lost by the narrow passage of Bristol Bridge; and yet no steps have yet been taken to prevent it – so attentive are we to the PUBLICK GOOD! Common Humanity and all the Benevolence so much boasted of in the present Age, should move us (one would think) to have the lives of our fellow creatures more at Heart, and make this opulent city immediately set about some effectual Alteration to secure us from such shocking Disasters, which (as wheel carriage have so much increased of late) daily become more frequent, to our exceedingly great Reproach.'

London Bridge was descried as [16] 'less a bridge than a causeway with culverts. Its piers blocked abut 45% of the river's flow at high tide when it was built, and more than that when the water level dropped below that of the protective barriers, or 'starlings' that were built to support and protect the piers. As the bridge got older, the starlings got bigger and bigger until by the 18th century, only 1/5 of the river could flow unobstructed under the bridge at high tide.' This was due to its poor construction; a wall of wooden piles driven into the river filled with rubble so when the wood rotted, more piles, so more obstructions, were added. There was even a saying, 'the London bridge was for wise men to pass over, and for fools to pass under.' It was more usual for boat passengers to disembark on one side of the bridge, then take another boat on the other side, rather than risk shooting the rapids. It was for this reason that the port of London grew downstream of the river. It is also the explanation, rather than climate change, for the Thames' famous ice fairs. These were possible because lumps of ice became lodged between the arches, allowing the river upstream to freeze solid. The last one

Page 2

was held in 1814 before the old bridge was removed. [17]

Bristol's port was originally upstream from the bridge; the city seal shows ships going through the castle water gate. An early drawing shows water surging between the arches during the 'fresh' as the tide went out. There were complaints at this time that the three massive pillars made navigation of ships difficult, and the strong current and high tides made collisions common. Whilst Bristol's bridge clearly presented problems to boatmen, they were still noted as passing through the arches, as when a boat hit the pillars and 4 men and a boy had to be helped to safety. The incident was noted as [18].'a boat struck again' suggesting this was not a rare occurrence. The problem seems to have been more the lack of height beneath the arches limiting the passage to small local boats in an age when ships were steadily becoming larger, as shown on John Rocque's map of 1740

Various surveys on the old Bristol Bridge noted the soundness of its masonry; the unknown builders had clearly known what they were doing. Missing from the debate, but recorded in the Chamberlain's Vouchers [19] are details of repairs to the bridge in the summer of 1741. Mason George Walker, then one of many working on the Exchange, was paid £33/4/0 for himself, 5 masons and 5 labourers for the work. John Webb received 10 shillings and 6 pence for the inconvenience of allowing them access through his house for 26 days. There were also costings for boat hire. Twenty tons of arch stones, 64 tons of wall stones and 32 bushels of lime were used, so this was a major repair, though seemingly on a single arch.

So the original bridge wasn't just well built. Any structure needs to be well maintained, and the above example, probably one of many over the years, suggests good local masons at a time when so many skills had been lost. It also shows, with the construction of houses on it, a commitment from the Corporation to maintain the structure, which makes their subsequent behaviour in regard to the bridge rebuilding even more strange.

Despite many writers claiming Bristol's economy slumped at this time, concerns were often noted of the overcrowded quays. In summer 1759 [20] a fire broke out on a Camarthen coaster on the Back, caused by a bottle of Aqua Fortis breaking. Only two berths away was a Milford vessel with over 3 hundredweight of gunpowder on board for His Majesty's forces. Understandably the residents of St Nicholas' parish were alarmed by the incident. So there was clearly a need for more berths for large ships, preferably upstream, a matter much debated by the Corporation and the city's merchants over the decades.

And there was the position of the bridge. The bend immediately upstream meant the force of the current was directed towards the quay near St Nicholas, tearing ships from their moorings during flood tides, so making the Redcliffe side safer. Some claimed the bridge was at the wrong angle to the current, further aggravating the problem.

Some would-be bridge surveyors claimed that the pillars were unsound, but no mention was ever made of the bridge falling down. The problem was a far more modern one: that of peoples' lives changing too fast for their environment. Initially plans were considered for pulling down houses on one side or the other, and extending the roadway without any major changes to the fabric, for which the suitably named James Bridges drew up plans and costings. Again they were probably looking towards the capital, as in 1757, the remaining houses on London bridge were taken down, the central arch replaced and the pillars refaced in the newly fashionable Gothic style, which extended the old bridge's life a further 60 years. But in Bristol the notion of altering the old bridge was soon buried beneath tons of new arguments. It was decided that they needed a new bridge, it was realised that the streets leading to it also needed widening, so the rebuilding act also carried provision to create wide streets of well built houses to replace the medieval wooden jungle. The higher rents from these were intended to help pay for the bridge.

The building affair coincided almost exactly with the Seven Years' War. And it can be no coincidence that the nation's largest merchant enclave, London, also saw their bridges suddenly prove inadequate. Merchants of both cities were great supporters of the War; there was even a riot in London against the peace-seeking king and his supporter Lord Bute [21]. Merchants of London, the thousands of watermen, and the parishes which could be forced to support them if laid off by the bridge, all actively opposed the proposed Westminster Bridge [22].

John Summerson noted "London is above all a metropolis of mercantilism. The basis of its building history is the trade cycle rather than the changing ambitions and policies of rulers and administrators. The land speculator and the adventuring builder have contributed more to the character of the Georgian city than the minister with a flair for artistic propaganda, or the monarch with a mission for dynastic assertion." [23]

If the above holds for the city of London it was even more true in relation to Bristol, so far from the Royal Court, but closer to the new trade and wealth of the American colonies. But the similarity with the capital goes further [24] "Bristol, like London, was essentially a two and not a three-class society in ordinary eighteenth century terms. There was a middle-class and a lower-class, but the old city could not boast of a noble or an aristocratic class." Many cities had a lord of the manor who made his presence felt, but though Bristol was ringed by aristocratic Berkeleys, Beauforts and Smythes, the real power lay with the independent merchants; none so rich as the fondly remembered medieval merchant princes Canynge or Norton, but many did well as the tide of affluence rose with the first economic boom since the collapse of the medieval wool trade.

The war saw an immense impact on business for Bristol. Whilst trade with the colonies became far more dangerous, the merchant ships were soon converted to privateering, so they continued sailing. Along the quays beyond the old city limits shipwrights such as the Tombs family and Sydenham Teast were kept busy building and repairing ships including Men of War, which kept sail and rope makers, anchorsmiths and chandlers busy. Sailors, marines and soldiers passed through the city on their way to manoeuvres or to the battle front, so victuallers, distillers, maltsters and brewers did well, as did the more obvious innkeepers etc. Supplies of munitions also passed through the port, with stores of gunpowder being a source of concern when fires, always a risk, broke out. Clothiers, weavers and bootmakers saw trade increase, supplying the men in uniform. We can almost hear the sound of coins clinking into the city's coffers. All these goods had to be moved about the city, to and from the quays and beyond, causing a major increase in traffic.

Page 4

But increases in trade did not just provide the means to build and develop. This new prosperity actually made major changes necessary. At the start of the century Bristolians still crowded within the medieval walls, walking, or - given the local alcohol consumption - staggering, to wherever they needed, and promenading into the surrounding countryside on Sundays. Even by mid century, the accountant and diarist William Dyer, whose work took him to London and Liverpool, hired a horse rather than owning one. But as the city spread beyond the walls along the river to the spa at Hotwells and up the hill to Kingsdown, houses for the newly rich were being built bigger and often included coach houses. Attending balls and entertainments at the Assembly Rooms or trips to Bath and the Hotwells definitely required proper transport. And for the even better off, the 1750s had seen a boom in building manor houses in South Gloucestershire.

These wealthy people needed feeding and entertaining, and to keep up with the fashions in clothing and house furnishings. Country people flocked to the city in search of higher wages, some to earn enough to emigrate; local and overseas trade soared. All of which increased the number of coaches, carriages, farm carts, brewers' drays, sledges and flocks and herds of animals pouring along the city's streets. The war played a major part in aggravating the problems on the bridge.

The city seems to have been full of ideas on what to do; one can imagine the coffee houses and inns abuzz with everyone suddenly an expert on surveying and engineering, or close friend to someone who was. As late as March 1760 ideas were still doing the rounds, some published in Felix Farley suggesting a single arch be used with the existing middle buttress as a temporary support, or to follow John Wood the younger of Bath's sensible suggestion, to take down all the houses and assess the structure before making any final decision.

But there is one which was only briefly mentioned in Felix Farley [25] which would have saved a lot of later problems. Following the report of yet another woman having her leg broken by a carriage, note was made of plans to build a bridge for heavy carriages only, from the top of Castle to Temple St. Since these heavy vehicles were the source of many of the bridge's problems, it made sense to remove them with the equivalent of a modern town bypass. Like today's heavy lorries, these vehicles were bringing in little passing trade but were interrupting normal business for local shops. Vehicles cost a lot of money, so their owners of carriages or huge wagons, must have been capable of paying tolls. This option would have meant there would have been less types of tolls, so less arguments over their fairness. It would also have removed the need for a temporary bridge, and the costly removal of houses on the old bridge, so saving many thousands of pounds.

The nearest city gate was that of St Nicholas, a notorious bottleneck where John Wesley fell from his horse: he considered it a miracle that his life was saved. But the gate was part of the fabric of St Nicholas' Church, on part of the old city wall. Whilst nobody disputed the need for the gate to be widened, an alternative suggestion to pull down adjoining houses to make a footway were ignored. Appeals were made from the parishioners to preserve their beautiful chancel, possibly the finest in the city, even though it had been falling down for years, and some 20 years earlier John Wood the Elder and the 'ingenious Mr Padmore', builder of the city's Great Crane, had been consulted on how to shore it up.

Thus, we are dealing not with the repair or rebuilding of an ancient bridge across a river with a huge tidal range and force, the engineering of which would have been difficult enough in those days. It was also more than the construction of a major public edifice, only the first since Wood's Exchange and which had caused so much dispute 2 decades years before. The bridge became a starting point, the focus for rebuilding and cleaning up the mouldering medieval heart of the city. By widening the bridge, routes to it became bottlenecks; when one was cleared, the obstruction moved on, causing a domino effect across the city. And once new stone buildings went up, the old wooden buildings, many of them repaired and shored up over decades or centuries, began to look increasingly shabby and threatening in case of fire. So this became a major exercise in town planning and rebuilding. But as with every exercise, mistakes were bound to happen.

Widening or rebuilding the bridge was clearly important by the 1750s, but finding someone with the necessary skills was daunting. The French, with trade routes through the high mountain passes were the first to establish a school of civil engineering, and the Welsh, with steep rocky valleys and high rainfall were building lots of bridges before losing many of them to floods. When Henry VIII dissolved the monasteries, he destroyed the religious patronage for the arts, and the yards where masonry skills were passed on. For almost 2 centuries in England it had been the age of the local carpenter. Few of England's rivers were raging torrents, at least not where people who mattered travelled, so travellers had coped with passage by ford or ferry for centuries. In London, vigorous opposition to any new bridge came from the thousands of watermen whose livelihood was threatened, and the parishes which would be forced to support them and their families if put out of work. Labelye made complaints of them deliberately running into the piers to delay his project. The country had no bridge builders because that, though complaints were made of delays and horses getting cold, they were not enough to overcome ignorance and vested interests.

As John Summerson noted when a new bridge at Westminster was being proposed, [26] 'Westminster Bridge was an engineering triumph in a capital which possessed no engineers'. Given the size and importance of the capital, if they had trouble finding suitable bridge builders, what hope was there in the provinces? But he continued, 'Bridge building in the 1730s was better understood by certain provincial masons than by anybody in London, except, perhaps, General Wade. It was still conducted very much on medieval lines by bridge-building families. No bridge had been built over the Thames in London since London Bridge itself, in the 12th century.'

When Bristol planned its bridge improvements, they had two recent models to consider. For Westminster Bridge, a French trained Swiss, Labelye, was imported. He was an expert on river and harbour works. [27] 'a man of a professional type which England had not yet learned to produce... Labelye set a standard which was recognised by Gwynn, Mylne and Smeaton, Telford and the Rennies; and his bridge was the foundation of an English tradition in bridge building second to none in Europe.' Labelye used pile-driving methods learnt from watchmakers and the radical new method of building wooden caissons, or coffins, which were floated into position and sunk to the riverbed to allow masons to build the pillars within them.

The other design was rather closer to home; the famous bridge at Pontyprydd. [28] It was built by William Edwards, a Non Conformist minister and building contractor; a massive act of faith by a man who was learning as he went along. He undertook to build a bridge that would last 7 years, which sounds easy but indicates the difficulty of the challenge. His first attempt on 3 arches was washed away in 1743, after surviving only 2 years. To prevent a repeat he decided to try a single arch, despite the fact that the span of 143 foot would make it the longest single span in Europe, a feat not attempted since Roman times. Floods carried away at least part of the timber supports, but he repaired them and the bridge was completed, though it is unclear how long for. The usual problem - that of the weight of the buttresses pushing out the keystone of the arch - led to its collapse. But his determination won him local support and a collection was made to help him continue. This time he included circular arches in the abutment, making the structure lighter, and further reduced the obstruction to flood waters.

Gwyndaf Breese's book on Welsh bridges lists this bridge under failures, which is reasonable due to the collapses, but in fairness, there is no mention of any injuries or fatalities in its construction, and it became a major attraction for those who had the leisure to go touring in Wales. Edwards, with his lack of formal training, showed a courage that was rare in professionals . And he more than achieved in his remit as the bridge survives today, unlike many constructions from that time, including Labelye's bridge which was replaced in 1861.

These were the main choices facing Bristol as it considered the future of its medieval bridge. Which of two beautiful, classical designs, and should they be on old foundations or to a radical new and risky design? In retrospect it seems the answer should have been easy after all, merchants tend to be conservative, guided as much as anything by the adage if 'if it ain't broke don't fix it'. They should have automatically gone for tinkering with the old structure. But Bristol was unusual in its absence of an aristocracy to step in an make big decisions. Instead they practised a form of local democracy which amounted largely to long, drawn-out arguments. Elections were often notoriously expensive, disputed affairs, and into the19th century the city was often cited elsewhere in arguments against expanding the voting franchise elsewhere. With so much money involved there were always going to be problems.

In London, Labelye's appointment is often said to have aroused much resentment [29] but most of the hostile pamphlets were published either before his appointment or after the disastrous collapse of a pier, which provoked the outspoken Batty Langley's famous pamphlet 'The Swiss Impostor' showing the engineer hanging from a gallows beneath an arch of his bridge. Labelye's appointment was supported by the Earl of Pembroke who possibly aided in design as well as attending most of the meetings from the outset. When the Earl died suddenly in 1750 Labelye thus lost the latest of his many early supporters. Claiming ill health, he left for France in 1752 and probably died in Paris in 1782. But at least he had seen his bridge through to completion.

CLEARING THE JUNGLE

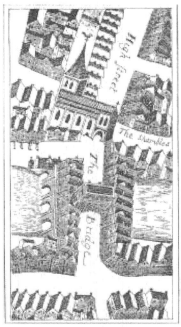

Bristol Bridge. From Beyer.

The Bridge was not just a means of getting across a river; it was a crucial part of a complicated property jigsaw in the commercial heart of the city. William of Worcestre, who despite his name, was a native of Bristol and a tireless pacer out and recorder of the medieval city. He gave several different measurements for the length of the bridge [1] so apparently he was confused as to where it began and ended. Even when a house was specified on a contract as being 'on the bridge' , vagaries of language meant it may have been anywhere on the line of houses which continued along the quay.

Descriptions of the old structure add further confusion. One writer stated that none of the houses encroached on the roadway of the bridge, i.e. that they were entirely hanging over the water on secondary arches, which may have been the case early on. But through the 16th and 17th centuries, houses had been repeatedly added to, and shop fronts extended to encourage custom. As the heights of buildings rose, so too did the need for storey posts to support the overhanging floors, which also impinged on the streets. With houses on the bridge being perhaps the tallest in the city, so too their overhangs must have been amongst the largest. The Common Council often had to deal with such obstructions. William of Worcester noted in 1480 that there were four cellars at the end of the bridge.

To further complicate matters, there were problems with establishing ownership. Some people owned houses, ie they held leases from the Corporation or Parishes, usually of up to 40 years duration. These were often sub-let in whole or part, and there are mentions of people with interests, or moieties, in properties, so it is often unclear who was actually living there, especially given how vague and out of date some of the records were. And when houses were being bought for removal, several Quarter Session records note that the tithe records of St Thomas, including the southern half of the bridge, were so lacking in detail that ownership could not be established, so payment for properties went into the Corporation coffers; the cash may still be sitting there.

Writers claim varying numbers of houses on the bridge, usually 27 or 30 but this is based on a very cursory reading of contemporary records, an understatement by half. The records of the Poor Rates for the parish of St Nicholas [2] which covers the northern half of the bridge, looks like a modern exercise book with striped card cover and good quality paper. It lists occupants street by street, with the rent they paid; some were noted as making private contributions to the poor, so paid less or were exempt. The first house was that of John Taylor who paid £20 per year rent for a property and a further £7 for a 'shop under the vestry' from which we can guess that Taylor was tenant of the old chapel house in the centre of the bridge. Rents varied from £7 paid by Thomas Lanyon to his neighbour William Williams who paid £24, so there was a fairly wide range, with rents above those of the nearby Shambles which went up to £14, but had been left behind by some of the grander houses on Queen Square which could go up as high as that of Henry Combe at £70.

The St Thomas book [3] is dark, and made of coarse paper. It is a long uninterrupted list of occupants and what they paid, with no attempt at breaking them into streets, so there is no way to separate the residents on the bridge from all the others. Whilst we know from other sources many of those who lived there, many, like William Dyer, apothecary had 2 properties in the parish, for which he was paying £16 and £20 per year. At one point he was renting a stable adjoining one of them and his neighbour Bassell Woods had a cellar, which makes it unlikely it was on the bridge, but if a camel could be kept on London Bridge, who can say what was possible. What this rate book does tell us is the parish included many industrial premises. Glasshouses, brewhouses, distilleries and warehouses had taken over the old weavers' premises with drying yards. They were often advertised for sale as being for 'any business that requires room'. More worrying, there were many void properties. Whilst rents could get as high as the £25 paid by Richard Nelmes or Thomas Cave's £22, many were in single figures. In crossing the bridge from St Nicholas to St Thomas' parish, one passed from a bustling affluent city to a region in long term decline.

The value of properties was initially assessed by a group of master builders, such as carpenter and architect George Tully, who was responsible for building part of Dowry Square at the Hotwells. Daniel Millerd had been carpenter on the Exchange and Post Office, and masons Thomas Manley, George and William Daniel often worked for the Corporation. These master builders often bought or were granted the materials of the old buildings they were taking down, so really knew the value of properties about to be demolished. If their assessment was refused, a jury was summoned to make further inquiries, sand their decision was then final. Despite the title of surveyor being applied to James Bridges, and his replacement Thomas Paty, they were never involved in these valuations.

The Act of Parliament [4] allowed not just for the rebuilding of the bridge, but also for 100 yards leading to it, so from the outset surrounding properties were targeted. The temporary bridge, just upstream, required space; cranes and building materials needed to be unloaded and stored. Properties were thus purchased in Baldwin St, The Shambles, The Back and High St, and across the river in St Thomas and Redcliffe Sts.

It wasn't just the Bridge Trustees that became involved in property dealings at this time; in fact they seem to have lagged behind private speculators. In December 1764 a gout or drain was laid from Bristol Bridge to the new houses in St Thomas St, though it is uncertain who built them.

Whilst St Nicholas' vestry complained of losing the income from wealthy parishioners on the bridge, no mention was made of similar losses on the southern side. In fact the local paper by Felix Farley rarely mentions events there, except for the occasional sale of the various, often large, public houses and coaching inns. St Thomas parish, had grown rich from the wool trade, like that of its mother church St Mary Redcliffe, but it had been in economic decline for some time. Centuries earlier they had been too poor to maintain their almshouse so permission was granted by Queen Elizabeth to hold a market there, a very early form of modern job creation, and later lost access to the Redcliffe pipe due to lack of funds. They must have welcomed the proposed improvements.

Another bout of speculation triggered by the building of the bridge and opening up the area was by Jeremiah Ames who later became mayor. In January 1766 bought up void ground in Dolphin Lane for the then sizeable sum of £400. [5] For many years they were known as the New Houses, but no details survive. We can only assume they were expensive. We know they were completed by February 1769 because Ames bought some more void ground next to the houses in Dolphin Lane, including [6] 'liberty to build over the well and pump (Trustees to build round pump and to first storey) leaving room to draw spears etc of the pump'. This must have been St Annes' Well, or St Peter's pump, moved to Stourhead during later road widening. This awkward sounding arrangement allowed the area to be developed whilst still maintaining the public water supply. So Ames developed the whole of Dolphin St from Wine St up to and including St Peters pump. Again, we have no idea what they looked like, but like all else that followed, must have been of high standard and quality build to justify the expense.

When the Exchange was built in 1740 the antiquarian Dr William Barratt commented on how wonderful it was to have such a large open space in the middle of a crowded city. The pulling down of the old bridge, and other houses must have been even more dramatic. For the first time, many Bristolians could get a clear view of their city's namesake. He talks of [7] 'opening up a free and unconfined prospect over the river and into the city and distant country, where the eye before was confined to a dark street (for much else was old or with houses on both sides)... all conspire now to render this a most pleasant spot, as well as an airy and healthy part of the city.' If the old city was a jungle, this was clear felling, and it was a good and necessary thing.

Enacting the Act

Although Felix Farley had been predicting action on the bridge affair since 1754, no real progress occurred until 1757 when the initiative was taken by Daniel Shewring, auctioneer, merchant and bridge resident who must have been fed up with having his front door open onto an early version of the M32. He commissioned a plan from architect James Bridges who had recently arrived in the city. This seems to have provoked action at last, and the Common Council of Bristol Corporation called a meeting on 28 August 1758 to discuss [1] 'complaints of obstruction and hazards there.'

In early November the Corporation formed the Bridge Committee, 7 men including the present and several future mayors, to meet every Tuesday evening to consult qualified persons, receive plans, proposals etc. for rebuilding and widening the bridge. So, though Bridges had made the initial running, nothing was decided at this stage, though he must have been the favourite to get the job. The following January these 7 reported they had been helped by Mr Bridges, carpenter and surveyor Mr Tully, and other workmen, as well as several lightermen, or boatmen.

The committee unanimously decided to the build new bridge on 3 arches according to Mr Bridges' plan on the existing foundations. It was proposed to raise money by a coal tax, a toll on carriages, horses and cattle, a duty on houses not more than 3 pence in the rateable pound, to be paid equally by tenants and owners, and an increase in wharfage both exports and imports. All of which seem straightforward enough.

Then a public meeting was held at the Guildhall where the Town Clerk read out the committee's decisions, together with schemes for raising funds, but many of the points could not be agreed upon, so a Citizen's Committee was formed, with one representative from each of the 24 city wards who were to meet with the Town Clerk to agree the proposed taxes. This committee included Michael Miller, solicitor and agent to MP Jarritt Smith. Many of them later held office for the corporation, several including Miller served as mayor, so they were hardly a bunch of radical outsiders. When John Wesley investigated claims of mistreatment of French Prisoners of War at nearby Knowle, a collection was made to clothe them. Many of these same men were on the committee to distribute the funds raised, so they were actively concerned with the. public good.

This Citizen's Committee was to present their decisions to a public meeting for further discussion, then publish their decisions in the local press to allow for yet more discussion. At the end of all these meetings and talks it was believed all objections would have been dealt with and a bill agreeable to all could go speedily into law. That was the plan, and a very fine one, if long winded and time consuming.

In March, 'A Citizen', ie James Bridges, published his 'Short Historical Account of Bristol Bridge' with his plans to improve it, and notes on other bridges in the kingdom and abroad. To encourage sales the profits were to go towards rebuilding St Weburgh's church which Bridges was supervising at the time and was struggling for funds.

It took almost a year before another public meeting was held, by which time several residents of the bridge had moved out. A fire broke out in December, burning the upper parts of several houses including the old chapel house which crossed the roadway in the centre. People lived in the upper parts of these buildings, with businesses on the lower floors so the fact that the source of the fire was unknown further suggests the emptying of the area. Soon after, on consecutive nights, haylofts of 2 public houses near the bridge on Redcliffe Street caught fire, so the neighbourhood seems to have either become very careless or uninhabited also. A negro, Landovery, stole some soap from Michael Miller, and sold it to Jonathan Adams, a grocer on the bridge. Landovery was transported for 7 years, Adams for 14 so it seems as the number of residents fell, so did their standards of behaviour. Limbs continued to be broken but Farley reported no more fatalities for a time.

The public meeting at the Guildhall agreed that the old bridge and avenues to it needed enlarging, and that a temporary bridge should be built on the inside of the old bridge before work was begun. Wharfage was to be included in the means of fundraising, as well as coal duty, house tax and tolls on temporary and new bridges to last 5 years. All of which seemed reasonable enough. But they also agreed to build a single arch stone bridge in case of damage to the temporary bridge. Somehow the plan had gone from merely pulling down old houses and extending the roadway to building no less than 3 bridges, 2 in permanent stone and a temporary one of wood. This seems utter madness, a complete break with the merchants conservatism the city was known for. As a writer in Farley's journal noted, this fear would make sense if the Avon were as wide as the Thames, or if there was a Waterman's Company to lobby against it, so the reasoning must lie with other vested interests. The man most frequently cited as being responsible for this scheme was John Wallis, local architect, and promoter of the single arch bridge to be built further upstream by the gloriously named Ferdinandino Stratford.

In early February 1760 the magistrates requested a further public meeting, and [2] 'the whole city was big with Expectation of a happy issue'. The committee hoped the Corporation would go along with them but the Town Clerk sent a message which destroyed whatever had been achieved by a year's meetings and consultations. Felix Farley, a great supporter of the rebuilding, did some serious ranting over this, yet again noting the loss of lives and limbs that delays were causing, urging all to put the welfare of their fellows and their city before petty private interests. He singled out the promoters of the single arch bridge at Hawkins Lane, ie Wallis & co, claiming 'several scheming gents... begin to be more and more sensible of the impropriety of that or any other [scheme]' Sadly his claim was premature.

After a year's discussions, it seemed all were in agreement to get the act passed so work could begin as soon as possible. But within weeks some serious opposition arose to the methods of financing and the corporation were considering deferring the matter till differences were settled. The differences between the corporation and the citizens became so unworkable the latter resigned in early March 1760 in order to act independently. They sent a bill of their own to parliament, rushing to catch the current session, which must have sent the corporation into fits of apoplexy.

MP Jarritt Smith noted that the publication of the bill seemed to have put the Merchant Venturers into a frenzy, and he was inundated with letters objecting to the proposed methods of financing. But even they were divided. A letter from Miller to Smith [3] noted there was much support for the wharfage fees, but that it came from 'most of them not one shilling involved in trade, those who opposed it ... [including himself] on whom most of that duty would have fallen which I declared was unreasonable and believe if they insist upon it, it will raise an opposition to bring the whole to nothing.'

The fact that these independents could even consider taking control of the project tells us much about the lack of local control by anyone person or body. It also demonstrates that there was a large group of wealthy citizens who were prepared to act independently of the Corporation. Their threat was real enough for the corporation to climb down on the coal tax in exchange for an increase in the house tax. Meantime, they made themselves available to discuss objections at the Bush Tavern every day except Sundays until the matters were resolved.

The situation was a mess. There were too many choices to be made and too many reasons for different groups to vote a particular way. Merchants objected to wharfage, people in southern parishes objected to bridge tolls, preferring them to be levied at the city boundaries. The coal tax was used to fund many of London's 19th century improvements such as public parks, but this was objected to as being hard on the poor. Westminster Bridge had been funded by a series of lotteries, but when these failed to raise enough, by annual grants from parliament. Barely mentioned so early were the disagreements over the design of the bridge itself, but these were doing the rounds, as well as which streets were to be widened and/or improved. Houses needed to be removed, ascents levelled, The Shambles, or old butchery area upstream from the bridge was cleared. It seems the bridge had opened the flood- gates for improvements that had been needed and discussed for decades.

Jarrit Smith claimed The Corporation charged through without proper consultation, but it seems these arguments could have gone on forever -they probably seemed to -with nothing being achieved. Meanwhile, as Farley kept noting, people were dying and being injured. Most of those injured were pedestrians, hence the poor, and he kept emphasising that despite this, all were at risk, and the costs would be felt by the well-off. That every man injured or killed meant an increase in the burden on local poor rates, which were paid by all householders, to support him and his family. A few decades earlier, when the city was smaller, rich and poor had lived much closer together. Notions of community and charity had been stronger, so such a reminder would probably not have been necessary.

Michael Miller noted that merchants and inhabitants over the bridge objected to the dropping of the time limit for the tolls to be collected, claiming ominously [4] 'it will never go down', that it would prove to be the basis of further problems 'as in effect this is the most unequal tax that can ever be thought of and in all probability would not end in 30 years'. Whilst few argued the rights of charging tolls on wealthy chaises etc, there was a clear bias against the citizens southern parishes of Temple, St Thomas and St Mary Redcliffe whenever they wanted to enter the main part of the city.

So at least 2 important people at the time saw real trouble ahead. But the Smith records claim that the corporation 'were more worried about the effect of delays in the bill, not the effect that such a tax would have on the people of Bristol.' The various petitions were holding up passage of the bill through parliament. The Corporation wrote to Smith on March 8 1760 urging him to get the bill through that season. Miller wrote to him the same day urging him to try to find other ways round the problem. Those living in the 3 parishes south of the bridge objected to the toll lasting over 5 years, the Society of Merchants wanted the coal tax brought back to discharge the debt sooner. The merchants also objected to the tolls, suggesting a larger land and house tax instead. Miller claimed the bill had been driven through with little thought and believed it would fail.

According to Seyer, the initial plans were for the bridge to be paid for by duties on coal payable at turnpikes, tax on homes and tolls for 5 years. He claims that [5] 'at the later end of March the bill came back to Bristol somewhat altered. Citizens were divided into parties on this occasion and spoke with great animosity.' Scores of pamphlets were published, only a few of which survive. The city was in uproar, but there was nobody with enough power to take charge. The affair seemed to bring out the very worst in the city, to reveal new fault lines. Everyone had their interests to promote: merchants trading locally had different needs to those making their money from the colonies, there were local artisans, industrialists, landed gentry and scores of middling tradespeople, residents of the inner city and those moving to the new suburbs beyond the old walls such as Redcliffe, Cotham and Clifton with fewer slums so local tax levels were lower.

At last the bill was framed, and with amendments it became law in May 1760 [6]. The tax on coal was dropped and the house tax doubled to 6 pence in the pound. The proposed 5 year limit on the tolls was also dropped; they were to continue until debts were paid off and sufficient capital raised to maintain the bridge. The last minute tinkering meant that the act was far from what most people wanted or expected. Smith managed to get more citizens appointed as trustees, thereby diluting the corporation's power but probably increasing the amount of debate and time taken over actions. It also meant that a larger quorum was required for meetings, and as the years passed and members died or simply failed to attend, this also created problems in getting anything done.

The trustees were given immense power to compulsorily purchase property and determine how new streets were to look so they could start to clear out the crowded old wooden city and build clean wide thoroughfares lined with fire resistant new shops and houses. They had given themselves the right to demolish a city gate, and with it, a parish church. The Shambles should have become redundant when St Nicholas' market was built 20 years earlier, but businesses there were still paying sizeable rents. Complaints were made of the blood and guts and dung left there, which, together with descriptions of the area being ruinous, encouraged their removal. Barratt claims the buildings were Gothic, and in the great floods of 1739 two of the buildings were undermined and fell into the river.

And there seems a massive contradiction within the act. It is incredibly vague as to the details of the rebuilding of the old bridge, and what it was to cost, indicating the matter was still to be decided. But it was crystal clear on the details and cost of the 2nd bridge, suggesting the designer was already chosen, possibly as consolation prize for having missed out on the main contract. It was to be a single span, to cross the river further upstream near St Peter's church, with an upper limit on its cost, so the trustees had fixed on details of a hypothetical bridge which was in the end never built, but still completely undecided on the bridge that was urgently needed.

To confuse matters even further, in 1758 Alderman Vick left £1,000 to build a freestone bridge over the Avon Gorge, later the site and initial funding of Brunel's Clifton Suspension Bridge. When mention was made of a single span bridge across the Avon, it was thus not always clear which of the two sites were being referred to.

Whilst there were plenty of gentlemen at the time doing the Grand Tour and coming home convinced they were the new Palladio, there is nothing to suggest the merchants of Bristol were wasting their time on such trivial pursuits when there was money to be made, especially during a lucrative war. So in the long list of men involved in the planning of the bridge, it is hard to find anyone with real knowledge or experience of building, probably due to a clause exempting any trustee from furnishing materials or being employed on it. Of the 113 Trustees named on the original act, only Thomas Paty seems to have been in the building trade. Of the Trustees Minutes of 1763, only John Wallis is noted as doing any surveying work for the bridge. It is unclear which of the various groups wrote which pieces of the final document. Despite all the haggling, it managed to resolve little. And in the vagueness of the details, was sewn the endless disputes which followed.

Building the Bridge

In view of all the time and effort put in by James Bridges, it seemed fair that he was appointed surveyor on 5 November 1760, by a comfortable majority. He immediately published his thanks in Felix Farley, adding 'I shall ever retain a grateful sense of confidence you have reposed on me; and that I shall upon all Occasions study a faithful discharge of my duty to the best of my abilities.' He also placed an ad asking for contractors for the temporary bridge, and the Bridge Committee voted him payment for his services to date, [1] 'a regard that does Honour to the Gentleman and his merit.'

This should have put an end to the squabbling, as it would safely be assumed that by his appointment as surveyor and approval for his design of the temporary bridge came acceptance of his design of 3 arches on old foundations. But that would assume the opponents of Bridges were gentlemen enough to concede defeat. Or at least that they were civic minded enough to allow the much needed project to proceed without further costly delays. But of course they were not. With the battle over The Act settled, the action moved on to the design and the designer.

An ad appeared in Farley [2] inviting applications from masons willing to take down Bristol Bridge and build a quay wall. From April 1762 the masons William Daniel and Thomas Manly were paid £700 for this, which was completed by July. The old bridge had 4 arches; the present one has only 3. Much of St Nicholas' pier was swallowed up by this new quay wall. On the south side, the Redcliffe wall was also brought out, making the new bridge considerably shorter than its predecessor, reducing the costs of stone to be purchased and also the risk of arches collapsing. James Bridges explained [3] he extended the cutwater of St Nicholas quay wall from the plan of 18 foot to 29 to lessen the dangers of the current against the bank, and enclosed an old slip 30 foot high and 6 wide to strengthen the quay wall upstream of the bridge

Barratt mentions that the Act for Rebuilding Bristol Bridge also covered [4] 'filling up the lower part of High Street thus making the ascent, before very great, much easier and more gradual.' This was not the first time the slope had been reduced. In July 1739 Common Council proceedings noted plans to lower High Street, that it was 'practical and very necessary to be done.' The lowering at that time involved moving water and drain pipes, re-pitching the road, carrying off 300 loads of earth and altering 50 doors. It proved so successful the wealthy inhabitants or Small Street, not wishing to be outdone, immediately arranged for their street to be similarly altered. When an archaeological dig was carried out in the area in 1975 [5] a stone building was located 5 metres below the present road level, so Bridges alteration contributed to this infilling.

Complaints made of stoppages on the bridge were often caused by the narrowness of the streets leading to it. One letter in Farley gave the example of carts loaded with goods from The Back near St Nicholas' church had to go up a steep slope, then turn a tight corner either into High Street or onto the Bridge, blocking passage for everyone else. So yet more houses needed to be removed to widen this intersection.

In August 1761 Farley carried an ad from James Bridges [6] 'All persons who are obliged to carry rubble or rubble mix'd with ashes to a greater distance than the Temporary Bridge to discharge their carts at the said Bridge, any hour of day'. The man was cleverly killing two birds with one stone. Despite the existence of several improvement acts, and the payment of contractors to clean the various parish streets, complaints, were often made of the amount of filth in the city. The booming population was largely to blame. Over the years, local papers often warned of prosecutions against anyone found dumping waste on empty ground in such as the long delayed Bridge Street, where old buildings had barely been cleared away when prosecution was threatened against anyone throwing [7] 'Dirt, Rubble, or Earth or any Filth' there.

But Bridges seems to have underestimated the amount of landfill the residents of Bristol could supply, or just the distance they were prepared to carry it, as John Wood, in a letter to the Commissioners [8] noted a number of extra expenses, including building the quay wall above and below the bridge on the north, ie St Nicholas' side, and the filling up of St Nicholas' arch 'which the materials sold [ie from the houses on the bridge] would have done very well, but now must be bought for that purpose'. Which probably refers to an item in the Chamberlain's account from the summer of 1763 [9] when £8/10s lighterage was paid for transporting slags from the Cupilo at Crew's Hole. This was waste from the large smelting works upstream on the Avon River, which was often dumped in the river, so causing navigation problems. A large quantity was used ill the construction of smelter William Reeve's famous black and white outbuildings al his estate of Arnos Court at Brislington, which was designed by James Bridges.

But Bridges also records [10] the building of a bay 'a little above the bridge' to divert the river round Redcliffe pier, whilst working on the Batterdeau and which also involved depositing slag. But delays meant cold weather prevented its removal, and currents blew a hole in the quay wall where no slag had been used, but was immediately repaired. He claims this caused a wave of rumours about the temporary bridge falling down.

In April Farley reported a curious event which people at the time must have understood, but leaves modern readers perplexed. They warned [11] 'that a certain Gentleman of this city have (sic) promis'd to pass 2 dice of equal cube and magnitude thro' each other, ten times in ten minutes.' A fortnight later, a full account was published, but clarifies little. [12] 'On Thursday last was exhibited to Publick view in this City the passing of two equal bodies of equal cube thro' each other 5 times in a minute: also a large cube thru' a smaller 12 times in a minute, to the. great surprise of all present, as it sufficiently proves, both in practical and speculative mathematics the falsehood of the old HYPOTHESIS, viz THAT SPACE AND MAGNITUDE CANNOT PASS THRU' A BODY OF EQUAL SPACE AND MAGNITUDE...This curious experiment was performed by Mr James Bridges, Architect and Builder of Bristol Bridge.'

Eighteenth century Bristol always seemed to have someone launching into extempore poetry to record noteworthy events, so this incident inspired an anonymous laureate: [13]

'Blush! Grecian, blush! To see thyself outdone
Blush at the Labours of thy British son;
Say'st thou the *larger* must the *less* contain?
Dost ask? Why *that's* to every blockhead plain.
Aha! Old Euclid's out; why, here behold,
This the least Die with ease the Larger hold."

This playing round with Euclid's rules must have been in response to one of the many attacks on Bridges, the commonest of which was that he lacked a liberal education and so knew nothing of the rules of geometry. What actually happened, we will never know. But it shows Bridges as a good natured showman. Several weeks later his actions were defended, suggesting his enemy was neither a [14] 'Gentleman, Scholar or Christian' before asking, 'Where lies the Folly of a few Friends to partake of an evening bottle (the conference of a wager).' Sounds like the definition of the 1960s, that is, if you remember what happened, you weren't there.

But the timing of this incident is interesting, as it was soon followed by his next, real stunt which was reported in May [15] 'After the Masons had work'd a few Days and Night (this week) on the cassoon of the New Bridge, it was floated to its place at High Water and sunk to the bottom of the River between some large piles drove for that purpose -The Diligence used by the contractors of this bridge is remarkable.

Like Labelye, Bridges was using caissons or wooden coffins to allow masonry work to proceed in the river; perhaps the first time this had been attempted outside the capital. This may well have been the factor that got him the surveyorship – few people must have had the knowledge to build this structure, and drive piles into the river to hold it in place. And it showed how experienced the local contractors were. But why were masons involved on the temporary wooden bridge? When eventually the materials were sold, this becomes clear; included were [16] 'the two stone piers on which it stands' So Bridges' design was a clever but functional hybrid.

On September 5 1761 Felix Farley reported that the Anniversary Feast of the Natives of the County of Gloucestershire met their President at the Taylors' Hall on broad St 'from whence they proceeded over the TEMPORARY BRIDGE made passable on this occasion (as a compliment politely paid by the society of Mr Bridges Architect and Messrs Evans & Collins the contractors) to the Parish Church of St Thomas.' Present were the Mayor, Sheriffs, the Duke of Beaufort from Badminton and his cousin Norbome Berkeley of Stoke Park, MP Jarrit Smith, Abraham Elton of local merchants dynasty, and 'many other gentlemen of distinction.' At about the same time, feasts were also held for natives of Somerset and the clergy but they were not similarly favoured. When the Duke of York arrived in Bristol the following January [17]. he was reported to have visited Queen Square, dined at the Merchants' Hall, entertained at the Assembly Rooms, then had supper at the mayor's house, all of which were within easy reach of the new bridge, but there is no mention of him visiting it or even noticing the wonderful new structure.

No pictures survive of the temporary bridge, but a brief account survives from a couple of visitors, one of whom later became a surveyor in Liverpool: 'went to see the new stone Bridge over the Avon 'tis a Strong Clumsy Bridge of three Arches and Ballustraded on each side, tis been 3 years in building and will take one year more to Compleat it There are 4 Towers or Boxes at each side the spring of the land arches.' [18] A local author records that the [19] 'carriageway was...30' wide, pitched with stone & there was a footway on either side made of planks so that as you walked you could see the timber work & the water thru (sic)the knots & joints of the planks. The footways were secured from the carriageway by a brestwork of boards. The temporary bridge was erected above the old bridge; 1 or 2 houses adjacent St Nicholas Gate were taken down to give good access to it.' This was the only possible site as St Nicholas' church was immediately downstream, and soon to be rebuilt.

Whilst it must have been a little nerve-wracking to see the water beneath their feet, the pedestrians must have felt safe at last, protected from vehicles. And the carriageway was quite an improvement on the narrow old bridge.

But what was welcomed by land travellers, doubled the problems or water transport, as Farley reported [20] 'a barge laden with coal passing though the temporary bridge ran foul of some of the supporters but by cutting away the Bowsprit, she swung though and struck on the foundations of the old bridge but by throwing out most of her cargo she got off on the next tide.'

Bridges complained of a collision with the piers [21] 'were the lightermen more careful in avoiding and running against the lower Braces I am persuaded nothing could damage it but Time and Fire'

The cost of the temporary bridge was [22] £2058/19/8, and in July 1766 Thomas Britton was paid a further £179 for repairing it. But before It was opened to thc public and tolls commenced on 1 January, there were complaints in Farley about the tolls, noting how unfair it was to charge [23] 'every brewers dray returning home with empty casks and glass bottlemen with their empty buckets and halliers with a few empty sacks in order to fetch provender for their cattle will be subject to the said toll which I heard from some of the Gentlemen of the Bridge Committee were never intended to pay'. The

Act of Parliament's wording on this shows how confused the situation was. Its exemption allowed 'no carriage, horse, or other Beast that shall pass over the said temporary Bridge or rebuilt Bridge when finished, loaden with coal, or returning unladen, or loaded with Grains only, after Delivery of such coal, shall pay any Toll or Pontage for passing either of the said Bridges.'

The tolls were numerous and complicated, apparently in an attempt to accommodate the wide range of users. Anyone refusing to pay the tolls risked having their carriages 'distrained'. and 'any person or persons who shall set fire to, burn, blow up pull down or destroy, either the said Temporary Bridge, the said Old Bridge or the said new Bridge,or any part thereof, or any works or Buildings which shall belong thereto or in any wise direct or procure the same to be done will be adjudged guilty of felony and suffer death without the benefit of Clergy.' Further, that 'All persons threatening or assaulting the collectors or interrupting them in their stations are for the first offence liable to a penalty of £5 or to be imprisoned 6 months.' [24] Turnpike riots had once been widespread in the Bristol area, especially to the east, towards the wilds of Kingswood, when such draconian measures had entered the statute books for the first time to punish those who smashed up turnpike gates and tollhouses.

The only record of misbehaviour at this time was a Mr Hetling, possibly the distiller, who paid a fine of £2 to the Chamberlain for insulting the Toll Gatherers [25].

In February 1762 James Bridges placed an ad in Farley for masons to work the stone for the new bridge, inviting them to view the types of stone to be used, and to discuss details with him. The contract went to William Daniel, Thomas Manley, Thomas Britton, William Evans and Richard Collins. The Daniel and Manley families often worked for the corporation; Britton had been employed repairing the temporary bridge, probably the paving, which suggests his area of expertise, though he also supplied the crane. Collins was a carpenter in St Thomas St, but no other work by him and Evans is known in the city.

Bridges' appointment should have stopped the arguments, but it seems it only fanned the flames of the opposition. Pamphlets were published, only a few of which survive, but the principal players of Bridges, Wood and Stratford, so we have only an inkling of the various exchanges. By June Farley was waxing lyrical in support of the surveyor. One reply to a pamphlet, [26] 'most unkindly calculated to injure the reputation of a modest man

ABOUT...how many years ago
Tell me chronologers, you know
When first Inanimates did walk?
anvils converse and sledges talk?
For in that time there liv'd a Greek
who knew right well what each did speak.
Quite convex was this learned sage
that is, lie bent, but not with age
and yet, 'tis thought, he had again
Ten times more sense than older men
to do him justice I'm not able
But as a sample, take this fable
THE VIPER AND THE FILE
A viper seeking some Repast
Came to a Blacksmiths shop at last
where wriggling up and down for awhile
he found a SOLID CUTTING FILE
At this he flew-would eat it up;

But gently sir; the FILE cries- stop
Then with compassion kindly said
I wish my friend you'd better BREAD
In vain you CHEW too plain to see
You hurt YOUR TEETH, you hurt not ME'

This was the second time this obscure Aesop's fable has been mentioned, and the references to ancient Greeks show the opposition hadn't changed its tune.

In August 1762 Bridges advertised for contractors to take down and rebuild St Nicholas' church according to a model. This is another aspect of the man's work: stone models were prepared by him for the main bridge and for the temporary one. Another survives from Royal Fort, one of the few clues as to its architect. Again, this suggests a thoroughness in his approach to his work, though Stratford also produced a model for the bridge.

A month later was advertised 'all the pewing, dish, pulpit and wainscot in St Nicholas' church'. Details were available from Richard Collins, carpenter, of St Thomas Street, so the same contractors were being employed.

In October a notice invited estimates for building a single arch bridge, and for a three arch bridge upon old and upon new foundations. So, despite all the hard work by Bridges, and the promoting of his plans by Farley, Wallis and others were managing to get a lot of support for Stratford's single arch plan. It seemed all Bridges had managed to achieve so far was to fill in St Nicholas' pier, bring out the quay wall to meet it and lower the High St in preparation for what was to follow.

The final decision was to be made at a meeting at the Guildhall on 1 November but this was adjourned, the final decision not being made until the end of December when bridges' plan of 3 arches was accepted but on a new foundation , which was clearly a compromise between the two groups leaving nobody the victor, nobody satisfied. Stratford and Wood had long maintained the old bridge was unsound, a decision backed up by Smeaton, but his opinion was based on Stratford's survey, without having visited the site so was of doubtful value.

A large number of local masons had given their opinion that the old foundations were sound. Caissons such as those by Labelye had worked well on his bridge, and the scheme required experienced workers, which Bristol clearly possessed. But the caissons sat on a layer of wood which would one day rot away, leading to shifting; piles to hold them in place had to be driven well into solid rock. The decision to build on old or new foundations was a huge gamble. Before Westminster Bridge was completed, one of its piers subsided. Problems continued till it was demolished in 1862, caused by a lack of piles driven beneath the piers, much aggravated by erosion of the Thames riverbed, by dredging and increased flow by removal of the work with Stratford. Bridges had complained of his large workload, and paid a clerk out of his own pocket, claiming [27] 'it is usual to have an assistant or foreman or pay extra on all large and public works'. He was being prevented from other business, but this joint role was clearly not what he was asking for. This definitely sounds like a compromise too far. Whilst the rebuilding of London Bridge had been done by two surveyors, [28] Taylor and Dance from 1757, they were not working in the centre of a professional storm such as Bristol had become.

Whilst workmen proceeded with pulling down old St Nicholas' church and unearthing stone coffins prior to rebuilding the church a whole 6 foot wider, the arguments continued. The Bridge Office sold off materials of houses which had stood in Redcliffe and St Thomas Streets, so the opening up of the ways to the bridge continued. Mid February finally saw a decision made. Bridges' plan or 3 arches on new foundations was accepted over Stratford's by a margin of 16 to 15 hardly, a resounding victory, but a victory nonetheless. It was enough to set Farley waxing lyrical yet again [29], this time in response to charges that Bridges' plan was unoriginal, which seems rather odd since a whole generation of architects including Burlington and the Woods had based their entire careers on copying classical designs.

Despite the earlier appointment of Bridges as bridge surveyor, this same meeting appointed him joint executioner of the

A NEW EPIGRAM UPON AN OLD PLAN
Should Bridges from Good Nature, vent such Lies
As --Neighbour Cymbal is most wondrous wise!
That he's an architect can out go
the great Venetian our Inigo
Or should he boast Vitruvius he'd out-do
and that Old Euclid was not half so true. .
This Compliance of his, would never pass
The tinkling cymbal, would be still an ASS
Again should Cymbal Palm it on the town
That modest Bridges' drafts were not his own;
That poor ignorant, Mistaken Man
Could never make, but always stole his plan;
This foolish Farce our Town would ill abide
And plainly will catch Scribbler that he lied.

It wasn't just regarding the bridge that Bridges was under attack. Claims had also been made that St Nicholas' church was unsound, so in March 1763 several experienced builders surveyed the foundations of the church, [30] 'when they were all unanimously agreed that the same were good, firm and sufficient that the walls were built on strong and permanent manner and in every Respect, be capable of supporting the intended Superstructure -After a long and careful examination, it appeared that the Report of the bad state and condition of the said foundation walls took rise from the wicked and ill designing persons to injure the reputation of a certain WORTHY GENTLEMAN.'

More sniping, more time wasting by Bridges' opponents. We have no idea how any work proceeded with 2 opposing captains at the helm. It is hard to imagine them working well together with so much mudslinging going on.

A week later another ad for contractors to build the bridge was placed by Thomas Symons, Clerk to the Trustees rather than either of the surveyors, suggesting whatever their roles had become, they were being marginalised. It announced that 'a proper person will attend every day ... to explain several parts of the plans' seems to distance them even further.

Then Stratford pulled a stunt to place him more in the public eye. He took an ad in Farley, front page, top right hand corner, utterly unmissable [31]

'Mr Ferdinandino Stratford, Architect & Engineer has lately taken an House with an Intention to reside in this city: he offers his service, as a contractor by the lump or as a surveyor of any Building whatsoever, whether on Land or in the AQUATIC ENVIRONMENT. He also executes all Sorts of Hydraulical Performance, professes himself an accurate Surveyor and Planner of Lands.

If any Gentlemen will honour him with their commands he flatters himself that he shall obtain their future favours and recommendations, as he is determined to make use of the most unwearied Application to preserve an incorruptible Integrity and study of all Prospects and true interests of his employers.'

All this time Bridges had been quietly getting on with his career in the city, never having needed to advertise his business, and being paid by the trustees to move from St Michael's Hill to The Back to be closer to the site, Stratford hadn't even bothered to move to Bristol. His name never appeared on any ads for rebuilding the bridge, so whatever his role he never was on a par with Bridges. This ad and its blatant positioning seems an act of desperation, from a man unable to win a fair race, now running out of ideas.

May saw contractors invited to remove the Batterdeau, or casings surrounding Redcliffe Pier, to be addressed to Mr Wallis on St Michael's Hill, or several other addresses. Again, there was no sign of the two surveyors who should have been supervising the scheme. An important meeting of the trustees was called, noting 'there is material business to be done, therefore the Trustees are desired to be punctual.' July saw a postponement for receiving proposals for the rebuilding.

At last the Bridge Trustees Minutes [32] provide a brief clarification. On 4 July they include a report scrawled by John Wallis following a 'cursory inspection' of the temporary bridge and lists the shortfalls in the agreed contract including a reduced number of iron grates for drains, substituting deal for oak. He claimed the bridge was weak and infirm in its original construction not thru' a want of Judgement of the General Framing.' He asked for an accurate survey of the temporary bridge to be made 'upon oath by strangers not citizens and by men of incorruptible integrity.' He claimed Bridges' work amounted to a shortfall on the contract of some £200, a serious charge of fraud.

Bridges' reply is incredibly detailed, covering 4 pages of clear, tiny print, dealing with each item in turn, ending with accounts of what he spent and what the contract specified, showing he spent £50 more than agreed.

He begins 'I am Sorry and Surprised that an Artist should be so blind or rather unjust to take the least notice of any of the articles of value placed in room of those omitted, especially as they are more useful, more numerous and more conspicuous. He claims the commissioners ordered the bridge paved which raised the surface so larger more costly drains were needed in the middle of the roadway.

Unlike Wallis's cursory report, Bridges is detailed and clearly upset at the smear on his reputation. Whilst his alterations seem numerous, they also show he was constantly responding to changes in conditions. Changes were not unusual in those days -Wren's plans for St Pauls' bear little resemblance to the building which now stands.

The motion for the survey was turned down, so an apparent victory for Bridges' but his application for extra payment was withdrawn.

By August the estimates were finally in, but were described as [33] 'vastly too large'. Contracts were submitted by Stratford for I arch of £9,500 and 3 arch for £12,000. Biggs & Ford, masons of Bath had an offer of 3 arches for £13,500, Manley, Britton and Daniel £11,500 and Evans & Collins for £11,980. So further estimates were invited for building a single arch, and a three arch span both on old and new foundations. The Trustees had changed their minds yet again. Wallis and his protege were steadily gaining ground. Bridges was still in charge of St Nicholas' Church, but it seemed he had lost control of the project he had put so much effort into. Then On 22 October 22 1763 Farley had a sad announcement

'To the mortification of many GOOD men, and to the Reproach of some that are not good, Mr James Bridges quitted this Town and sailed to the West Indies last week -No man was ever better beloved, and no man more deserved it, and consequently, in his Turn, no man more maltreated. ...I do not doubt but that many who treated him ill some months ago would some months hence be pleased at his Return; he was, as Shakespear says, TAKE HIM FOR ALL IN ALL, I KNOW NOT WERE TO SEE THE LIKE AGAIN: besides his being well hackney'd in the ways of men, that is, he had seen the World, he was a sincere Friend, and a pleasing companion: As to his Business, that of an Architect, his buildings are elegant and sound that fine, finished Edifice of the Fort [ie Royal Fort, home of magnate Thomas Tyndall], with which everyone is delighted, that religious one, now raising on the banks of the Avon in Bristol [ie St Nicholas], whose Beauty and Regularity will be the Object of our admiration when finish'd, speak greatly to his Advantage. But to crown it all, notwithstanding the united force of his Enemies, his Plan for the Bridge upon the Old Foundations will in succeeding times shew the man when his enemies are forgotten. As to those stinking vapours... Envy Infamy which his merit raised, they are now dispelled and scattered like an unwholesome Dew

> For Virtue, like the sun oppress'd makes known
> Th' opposing Bodies grossness – not its own
> Dispels that Gloom, that once obscur'd its Ray,
> And with redoubled Lustre gives the Day

As to the Commissioners or trustees of the Bridge, gentlemen who were absorb'd in trade and were not idle enough to mind any BUSINESS but their own: These (Mr Bridges says of THEMSELVES) never used him ILL but rather the reverse. But as 2 or 3 men of great consequence (as they thought themselves) tho' of little skill in Architecture, of these he says he has received the basest Treatment. For tho' they did know but little of the science, they took the direction of the whole upon them, saucily saying in the Kingdom of the Blind, we that have one Eye ought to Govern.'

All the backbiting finally proved too much, and the talented architect/ engineer vanished into the sunset. Farley's praise of him was clearly heartfelt, and probably shared by many in the town. Bristol seemed to have a real affinity with Hamlet, so comparing Bridges with the Prince of Denmark would have been understood as the highest possible praise. His mention of two or three unnamed gents who had caused so much trouble further confirms the support Bridges enjoyed, but it is hard for anyone to stand up to what seems to have been such a prolonged battle fought on so many fronts. A week later further clarification of the affair was printed[34]:

'No man can be more jealous for the Honour of his own city of Bristol, the Place of my Nativity... it is the second in our isle in commerce and should be the second in Reputation in other Respects: but I am afraid, that this foolish management of the Bridge Affair will for some time not drown but sink our reputations and our citizens cannot praise that Bridges that has not carried them safely over. The meetings of the Trustees have been in number too great amount, but to so little Purpose that over 76 adjournments ...they could agree to have nothing done. Had they come to Mr Bridges' Scheme at first, then he honestly advised them for the best, the Bridge had, e're this, been more than half finished. Besides, they have missed two very fine summers for the business: for the Avon was never so low nor the tides so weak as they have been these 2 years.'

It seems extraordinary that 2 or 3 men could have caused such disruption to a scheme so necessary to the city. But the 18th Century was a time of immense change, when the old certainties of the medieval world were giving way to the brave new world of empire. Bristol was ruled by merchants, the voters were mostly middling sorts of traders and tradesmen. Building skills were passed on through apprenticeships or by reading the right books. If a man claimed to be an expert, there were few qualified to challenge him.

The men who formed these committees, who accepted submissions and debated their merits, were seldom young, often had little knowledge of building, and they took time out of their busy lives to attend meetings. The battle for control of the bridge was not what they would have expected, and few would have had the energy to endure the endless slog of meetings, the arguments and counter claims. The conflicting details must have made their heads spin. Given the ignorance of building and surveying in England at the time, even by some so-called professionals, the only way ultimately test any one of the schemes was simply to go ahead and build it.

Farley had no doubt who was to blame for the departure of the bridge surveyor, and pulled no punches in his condemnation. [35]

'Genius of Bristol! Come thy poet aid
Help me to pierce the more than midnight shade
snatched from the deepest cell of Infamy
Hang Jacky's wash up on Day's broad Eye...
Jacky, black envy imp'd his wing, arose
(To art's fair Family and he were Food?)
He call'd -his pale-lipp'd brethren hear the noise
and came, obsequious to the wizard's voice
From each, the narrow soul each other caught
Not one o'er strayed into generous thought
...Jacky, proceed with unremitting Rage
with science still eternity warfare wage
with haughty mien, and supercilious Note
O'er all her sons extend Oppression's Rod
Pursue each fair design with ceaseless Toil
and Daw-like deck thyself with borrow'd spoil
so shalt thou gain thyself a deathless Name
and Grub Street Bards shall gibbet thee to fame'

Jacky Wall is clearly John Wallis, summoning up powers of the underworld to defeat good, but what does this say of the men who supported Bridges? Were they bewitched or just weak? An Epigram followed, 'The lame lawyer and the very lame architect'. No name is given to the lawyer but there was a lawyer at the time, who famously hobbled about on sticks, so he was probably one of those noted by Bridges as his attackers. To modern readers, all this anonymity seems odd, Bristol was still a small city, and readers would have understood the references.

By mid November, the Trustees decided to build a 3 arch bridge, and a further meeting was announced to decide on whether to use old or new foundations. A long detailed letter from tradesmen was published, in response to Mr Wallis's speech to the Commissioners at the Guildhall on 7 November. It began [36] 'As Mr Wallis is a Commissioner, he always has it in his power to impeach the Knowledge, Judgement and Experience of others, who he well knows, cannot be present to answer for themselves, as the Business of these meetings is always done in private; he likewise takes care to be always provided with some written trifling schemes, entirely to confute the business of those meetings, instead of assisting the gentlemen in bringing it to a decision, otherwise we believe the Bridge would have been half built by this time.'

So at last there is an explanation as to how Wallis managed to cause such disruption; but no motive. This letter was signed by no less than 13 local builders including respected master masons Thomas Manley, Robert Comfort and William Daniel. Unlike much of the propaganda, by attaching their names to their words, we have what seems to be a refreshing breath of honesty and some clear facts. They refuted Wallis' claims that the pillars were damaged, claiming 'the foundations under the Old Pillars must be extremely firm and good, to bear such a weight, as the old foundations did; more particularly the small counter Archers that bore the great weight of those immense pillars of buildings, together with their stocks in trade, and all materials for many hundreds of years, without the least settlement which must be supposed to be 10 times greater, than the weight of the new intended bridge.

Some more clarity here – the masons are suggesting the houses were mostly on the secondary arches, the stresses of which were passed onto the old pillars. So it is clear that whoever built the old stone bridge had done a thorough job of it.

They also note Wallis's accusation that the masons were afraid of going down to solid rock to build on new foundations. This they are willing to agree to, noting the dangers of excavating so close to existing structures; such as the Redcliffe quay wall and the temporary bridge. 'No man, that has either reputation or fortunes to lose, will attempt at any such riskque(sic), neither bring their friends as Bonding...'

The workmen noted Wallis's quoting Woods, Stratford and the late Tully, but only the parts that suited him, and his conclusions were seldom consistent, in one instance advocating large stone for a job, the next demanding small for the same. Likewise, he ignored the opinions of local masters such as themselves, as well as those of Londoners Mr John Phillips and Mr Shakespear who had been brought in as consultants by the commissioners and who claimed the old foundations to be sound.

They end their report with a robust defence of their own skills: 'Mr Wallis ... says that a few ordinary tradesmen who through want of a liberal education can be little judges of Architecture: why, what education is it to building a strong wall? We can modestly assure him there are as good masons and engineers in this city as Mr Wallis or Mr Stratford. Without vanity much better. The first has been a surveyor over a large circular stables which, of course must be of infinite service to the city the other has been a surveyor of the building of barns and farm houses, but as for his capital buildings, we should be glad to be informed where they lye.' These are hardly the words of ignorant men, and further underline the bad behaviour of the promoters of the single bridge.

They concede Stratford's skill in land surveying and describe him as a good workman, but question his behaviour in originally quoting £20,000 for building the bridge, then dropping to £12,000 by changing the type of stones used, so confirming he was to be the builder of the second bridge.

By early December, yet another pamphlet was promised to be published speedily, on the history of the bridge, claiming Wallis seemed to be on his journey to the Valley of the Shadow of Death, hoping he will repent. Then the comments went beyond what modern papers would tolerate, with [37] 'can you imagine when the gripes are on you, that by squirting at the street-door you defile my house; no, my poor boy: But be assured, that the whole town laughs to see me every Saturday rub your nose in it.' Farley's journal was published Saturdays.

It is unclear if this pamphlet was ever published, but after this the whole affair seemed to grow quiet. Everyone involved must have been thoroughly sick of all the arguments, and merely wanted the scheme to be completed. The Seven Years' War was over. In London the common hangman had burnt copies of radical politician Wilkes' newspaper North Briton. Post war unemployment meant that the region was beset by highwaymen and footpads.

Bristol was seized with an explosion of improvements, with schemes for building a new passage from the end of Corn St to the Quay, the new theatre on King St (now Theatre Royal) was about to commence building, and plans were afoot to build a new floating harbour, one of many such schemes which never proceeded. No announcement was ever made of Bridges' replacement or how the decision was made, but the Trustees' Minutes show Thomas Paty was giving them advice from November. On 5 December he was appointed Bridge Surveyor from I January for 100g per year. But the ad in April 1764 to build St Nicholas' steeple notes it will be based on a plan 'now in the hands of Mr Thomas Patty' so it is unclear who was the architect.

The vote was at last taken, and carried for the old foundations 45 to 18. Bridges was vindicated at last. The contract was awarded to Mess Britton & Ca for an estimate of £ 11,000. The ultimate losers were not Stratford and Wallis of course, but the city as a whole.

Gentlemen, Players and a Giant Travelling Clock

Unlike the other players, James Bridges of the contemporary record is a man of mystery, of unknown origins, an apparently single man who arrived in the city, designed several buildings, then headed off into the sunset, the Pale Rider of Georgian Bristol. Some sources suggest he was an American, but there is no record of this; he merely mentioned he had travelled there. He was alleged to have built a church in Philadelphia, but his pamphlets only note he had travelled there and seen a church that would be suitable to build in the middle of Queen Square, one of the options for the rebuilding of St Nicholas. He is always referred to as being from the city, which probably meant he was a local ratepayer. He never became a free burgess or freeman, so was not a tradesman or a native of the city. He lived in the parish of St Michael's, just outside the old city centre, a favourite area for those in the building trade such as the Daniels family of masons and mason-carver James Paty, who built the model of the bridge for him. Bridges was a common enough West Country name, from James Brydges of Hereford who rose to become the fabulously wealthy Duke of Chandos, and another of the same name was an attorney who lived to the east of the city.

No record exists of his having worked outside Bristol, and he made no claim to any work history in his writings, yet it is impossible that an unknown, untried architect surveyor would have been trusted with such a major project. He must also have had considerable wealth or -more likely -have affluent friends who trusted him, in order to have raised the bond for his work. In 1763 when Paty was appointed Bridge Surveyor he provided a massive £10,000 bond. One source [1] accused him of being a carpenter and joiner. But he declared the old wooden tower of St Nicholas church to be sound, when it proved to be ruinous, so he lacked practical building experience. And no journeyman ever earned enough to do the sort of travelling or develop the social contacts he seems to have possessed.

He appeared in the city about 1756, and in 1758 he rebuilt St Werburgh's church; there was a Bridges family in the parish, but he claims in one of his pamphlets he was not a parishioner. He designed two houses for Redland Court which were to be rented out to pay the vicar's living, but these have long been demolished. His wonderfully ornate fireworks display for the coronation of George III on Queen Square was a highlight of that exhausting public celebration. A model survives by him for the grand, Capability Brown style mansion of Royal Fort, now part of the university, which is generally accepted as proof that he designed it. Arnos Court's designer is unknown, but suggestions that parts of St Werburgh's church were included in the castle have led to the assumption that he designed this classical – gothic estate on the outskirts o the city. Both properties show genuine, unconventional talent. Linked to the bridge rebuilding, Bridges supervised the demolition of St Nicholas' Church, and designed the new one.

He seems to have been a very learned, skilled, personable man who travelled much but had little if any practical building experience. He mentions [2] 'I have examined a great many of the works of the Antients, such as temples, circuses, theatres, triumphal arches and bridges...' so he may have done the grand Tour as well as the American colonies. His submissions to the Bridge Trustees were incredibly detailed. He travelled the countryside talking to farmers and testing the stone from their quarries. He went to Pontypridd to view William Edward's famous bridge but decided it was mostly for pack horses and pedestrians, and would not stand up to the heavy traffic In Bristol. He was also keen to learn and to obtain expert advice. His report in the Trustees Minutes includes mention that he travelled to London to consult the 'ingenious Mr Mylne', and asked him to provide a plan which he declined, saying it was too much of a risk, but the great man offered to consult if the Trustees asked.

Still concerned about the design, Bridges went again to London, this time to see Sir Isaac Ware of HM Board of Works. Bridges claimed he 'treated me with great candour and was very ready to assist me and was pleased to say some very Kind things about the Plans laid before him and after obtaining all the satisfaction I could expect he was so genteel as to decline accepting any thing for his trouble saying the pains I had taken merited his Assistance and every Acknowledgement.'

Wood the Younger noted that Bridges' classical designs were often less than correct, confirming his lack of formal training, but to his credit, Bridges readily made the suggested alterations so was amenable and willing to learn. And when Ferdinandino Stratford was getting on his high horse about his own expertise, Wood seemed at ease siding with Bridges, the gentlemen architects against the spluttering contractor. He clearly got on with locals, was hard working and respected by many. Farley seems to have been convinced the attacks on him were futile, and did much to defend the man's reputation, as with the following [3]:

AN EPIGRAM FOR THE PAMPHLETEER
Tell me, good Sir, why all the ROUT?
and why this snarling? What's about?
Must he be conjuror or witch
That throws a Bridge across a ditch?
Thy wooden Pamphlet makes me laugh
who rais'd the beauteous Bridge o'er Taff?
An honest, unlearn'd Cambrian did
who never one page in Euclid read
Yet ages shall this Building see
When envy lies intomb'd with thee.

What is now known about James Bridges is stranger than any fiction. He was the eldest son of Henry Bridges of Waltham Cross, architect and builder of the amazing Microcosm Clock. This 'Matchless Pile of Art' was [4] 10 feet height on a 6 foot base, and showed, from the top, 3 alternating classical scenes, then an astronomical clock housed within a classical temple, with dials showing both the Ptolemaic and Copernican systems in action probably the only such combination, then a landscape with ships and carriages moving across it, and at the base a working carpenters' yard. It also housed an organ which could play mechanical music or as a stand-alone instrument. An early print shows the incredible structure flanked bon the right by Henry Bridges, and on the left by Sir Isaac Newton who checked the mechanism.

Bridges' clock was not the first to combine science and entertainment in such a manner, but [5] 'The importance of Bridges' Microcosm... lies in the nature of its displays (combining pictures to attract the multitude with educational and astronomical models) and the widespread publicity that accompanied it on its travels. Few, if any, other curiosities exhibited to the public in the 18th century can have had so much 'exposure' ...It must have provided provincial clock makers with an opportunity to see and examine a more complex mechanism (it was said to incorporate 1,200 wheels and pinions) than would normally have come their way.' But its appeal went far beyond clockmakers. This was the great age of discovery, and many people with the money and time were tinkering with science, and such exhibitions provided a focus and stimulus for their research.

RL Edgeworth, pioneering educator and one of Manchester's 'Lunar Men', a group of scientists and industrialists, visited Chester in 1765 and like many who could afford it, he visited the Microcosm. His memoirs describe [6]...'the machine represented various motions of the heavenly bodies with neatness and precision. The movements of the figures, both of men and animals, in the pictures, were highly ingenious. I returned so frequently to examine them, that the person who shewed the exhibition was induced to let me see the internal structure of the whole machinery. In the course of conversation, he mentioned the names of some ingenious gentlemen, whom he had met with at different places where he had exhibited, and among the rest he spoke of Doctor Darwin, whom he had met at Lichfield. He described to me a carriage which the Doctor had invented. It was so constructed, as to turn in a small compass, without danger of oversetting, and without the incumbrance of a crane-necked perch. I determined to try my skill in coach-making, and to endeavour to obtain similar advantages in a carriage of my own construction.'

The clock's travels have been partly traced from newspaper advertisements over 4 decades, when it was seen in England, Scotland, Ireland, and the North American Colonies. At Henry Bridges' death in 1754, he believed his son James, presumably with the clock, was in Antigua. His will [7] left his house to James, suggesting he was the only one who had come of age. The clock was left to his children David, Thomas and Sarah; in the case of any dispute it was to be sold. It is unclear when the Bridges family sold the clock, but when James arrived in Bristol in the late 1750s he may well have been looking for a change of career, and moving into architecture would have been a sensible option. In the Bridge Minutes Bridges makes a fleeting mention of his family, which may suggest why he wished to give up a life on the move. The Bridge Minutes include a brief mention by Bridges of a family, suggesting a reason to stop his life of travelling. The clock seems to have ended its travels in early 1775 [8] when it was billed second to a pair of musical temples; but after several weeks the microcosm, due to its popularity, was given top billing, which suggests it was, after an extraordinary 40 years on the road, nearing the end of its lifespan. It then vanished from record, till 1919 when the clock mechanism was found in Paris and is now on display in the British Museum.

This clock explains much about James Bridges. It tells us his father was a highly talented scientist and designer, so probably passed much of this on to his son. The clock gave James the chance to travel widely, to visit many important buildings, and seems to have earned enough to allow him to mix with the upper layers of society. Edgeworth's memoirs also hint at the clock being a focus for education. It must have drawn local scientists and dabblers together, to examine the structure, discuss it, and exchange information, so James seems to have thus gained access to some of the most cutting edge research of his day. Being a travelling showman, he needed good negotiating skills, the ability to communicate well, and this would have helped with his learning. Milbourne mentions later drawings of the clock included a cometarium added in the course of its travels, so it seems it was updated as new astronomical discoveries were made. Edgeworth's response to the clock suggests the impact it had on local people, and as a stimulus to research when cutting edge science was largely in the hands of so-called amateurs.

It seems James Bridges may well have been, like Labelye, one of that breed of professional type that Summerson noted did not exist in England in the 1730s. Twenty years later one had apparently appeared in Bristol, which makes him one of this country's pioneering civil engineers as well as an architect of great skill and style. His knowledge of fireworks and his birthplace of Waltham Abbey, home to the gunpowder works also raises questions about his family business being in armaments. Then, as now, munitions manufacturers were secretive, cutting edge engineering. It is the city's eternal shame that he was treated so shoddily. In the absence of any evidence of his work in the colonies, we must assume he met an early death there, like so many other young men seeking their fortunes in the New World.

It is hard to see John Wood the Younger as a rival to Bridges, as he seems to have had little interest in the project, though he did on several occasions become involved in discussions. The John Woods were the most famous architects in the region, nationally recognised, and towering above their provincial competition. Wood the Elder had been consulted when St Nicholas' church tower had been on the brink of collapse several decades earlier, and was given the contract for building the Exchange, but only after many others including Ralph Allen had refused the offer. The disputes and delays on this, Bristol's first major eighteenth century public building, especially the rivalry between Bristol and Bath workmen made him swear he would never work in Bristol again. So it was not surprising that when his son submitted a plan for the bridge, he showed little enthusiasm, but claimed he was very busy at the time.

He clearly saw himself as a better architect than any other involved. [9]: 'I couldn't help smiling to hear Mr Stratford mention symmetry and proportion of Palladio... The front of Mr Bridge's design was as little consistent with Palladian beauty as Mr Stratford's Paragon.' Despite this, the Commissioners seemed to have quickly dismissed his plans for a single span bridge as not worth looking into.

In view of later charges of corruption, a small incident is worth noting from the Trustees Minutes [10] 'Mr Wood acknowledged the purchase made by him at the last meeting was for Thomas Symons. Ordered that such ground be conveyed to John Symons a trustee nominated by Thomas Symons.' Thomas Symons was the Clerk to the Trustees from the start. Even by 18th century standards, this selling of land to himself and then conveying it instead to his brother, a surgeon and property developer in Bath, seems rather dubious. But the involvement of Wood suggests he built them, so explains his availability for advice to the trustees.

John Wallis was the name that kept appearing as the main trouble-maker in this affair. He was an architect and builder who lived near the Royal Infirmary, and was held in high esteem by some, but more particularly, by himself. Wallis's main claims to fame were the large ornate Circular Stables near Stokes Croft, and a wall he built on Durdham Down in 1746 which seems to have stopped runaway horses and stray sheep falling onto the rocks (his name may have been transformed over the years to become Sea Walls). Whilst this may well have saved the some lives, it scarcely justifies the apparently self penned claims of [11] :

'Let Cook and Norton tow'ring follies raise
Thy wisdoms, Wallis, will I sing and praise.
...Wallis observ'd with sympathising pain
when, fierce steed had scorned the feeble rain
and borne the rider, shudd'ring o'er the plain
soon resolv'd, as soon as his wall is seen
and we in safety now sweep o'er the green'

It takes a very cruel man to inflict such poetry on the masses, even then. And the fact that he eulogised himself strongly suggests nobody else would.

Since the Bridge Committee meeting minutes before March 1763 do not survive, it is unclear how he managed to wield so much power on the Bridge Committee and create so much damage to the project. But Bristol was still a small place and many tradesmen hoped for work on the bridge so were excluded from being trustees. Thus anyone with such skills who did offer their services would have wielded immense power. Farley frequently mocks the ignorance of the barn builder, but it is hard to tell whether he is referring to Wallis or his favourite, Ferdinandino Stratford.

While the public behaviour of Bridges and Wood seems to have been civilised enough, there is something rather unnerving about these two. Wallis refers to the Avon as [12] 'such a dirty low River is not to be matched in the Kingdom and consequently no elegant building ought to be placed thereon, to draw the public attention to it. Let strength and convenience be the only objects!' Which raises the question, why did he become involved?

But if local pride was not his strength, neither was diplomacy. In response to Bridges taking advice from local masons on the soundness of the old piers, Wallis responds: [13] 'doth he not know that men who can scarcely write their names and who are totally unacquainted with figures, are by no means competent judges of matters of this sort?' One hopes he never had to call on them to mend his house in a hurry. And there was a real moral problem in Wallis so publicly supporting Stratford and his plan. As the masons noted in their survey of the bridge pillars, their report was public, whereas the meetings of the trustees were closed.

Finally, there was the rival bridge builder. These days, a man called Ferdinandino Stratford would have to change his name or become a pop star. It is hard to discover how he made a living; his desperation in this matter suggests how underemployed he was. As a means of ensuring work was completed safely, accurately and on time, a bond was generally demanded from tradesmen at the start of a contract. When Stratford was questioned if he could provide security, he said he [14] 'would find workmen masons and carpenters who would undertake the building of it and give security for its execution.' This sounds worryingly vague and suggests a man with few connections or sources of funding.

Like many Bristolians, he was originally from Gloucestershire and he seems to have at least tried to make a living in the lucrative field of property surveying. His plan was, like Wood's, for a single span bridge, which would allow large ships to pass upriver, so extending the crowded quays. Like Wood, he also maintained the foundations of the old bridge were rotten. He was the only one who claimed the existing bridge was at the wrong angle to the river, so proposed moving the southern edge upstream some 18 foot.

But like his supporter, he didn't seem to excel at people skills. When he attended a discussion with Bridges and Wood, he accused them of being ignorant of how to handle large stones and stormed off. Wood is magnanimous: [14] 'I still confess inexperience in the mechanical executive of sinking to the rock for the foundations, but I imagine I am as much a master of the theory as Mr Stratford himself; and am sorry he by so trumpeting forth his own abilities as Mr Bridges and myself never once entered into the consideration of a method of work under water, through a tendency for Mr Stratford, who proposes to be a *Contractor*, lest we should discover to his prejudice , any part of the excellent methods for doing the work. It is the Contractor's business to perform their undertakings and find out means to do it. It is sufficient for you to know, gentlemen, that it can be done.' And if that did not put Stratford in his place, Wood continued [15] 'It is very kind of Mr Stratford to caution you against the unfair Dealings of some Surveyors; and at the same time very prudent in not giving even a hint of he many tricks of all contractors, which it is the duty of the Surveyor to detect.'

Silent Opening

On March 31 1764 Felix Farley's Journal announced that the foundation stone of the bridge would soon be laid, then on 7 April they announced it would happen the following Monday.

Then nothing.

No ringing of churchbells, no fireworks, no processions, no cannons booming, no cannons booming across the city, no riots, no drunks being fished out of the river.

When building commenced on John Wood's Exchange in 1740, the city turned out to celebrate: church bells rang, there was a grand procession and the foundation stone was laid with coins beneath it for good luck. Citizens jumped on it, to ensure it settled and vast quantities of alcohol were provided.

In 1752 the mayor and aldermen with other dignitaries went in a procession of coaches to lay the first stone for the new church of St George on the outskirts of the city. Even as late as 1851 when a new High Cross was erected on College Green, a grand procession made its way to lay the first stone. Westminster Bridge's first stone was laid by the Earl of Pembroke, with guns and fireworks. [1]

But on the opening of the new Bristol Bridge, there was a resounding silence.

Thomas Paty was paid £105 per year as surveyor [2], and in December 1763 the masons William Daniel, Thomas Manly, Thomas Britten, William Evans & Richard Collins were paid their first instalment of £2,000 for rebuilding the bridge. By the following August they had brought all the piers and abutments up to an agreed level. In December 1764 Thomas Briton received over £91 for putting up cranes and the contractors had got the piers ten foot above the low water mark, so despite all the claims that the piers had been sound, there was a lot of rebuilding after all, and a lot of waiting for stone, because a gap of two years then followed in the accounts. In February 1767 boatmen where warned to use the central, St Nicholas' arch not that of St Mary Redcliffe. June 27 saw Farley announce the central and final arch was laid the previous Thursday, and he hoped there will be no delays to its final completion. Trustee minutes [3] note action being taken against contractors 'in not compleating the Bridge and not leaving Mr Vaughan's quarries in workman- like manner.' From August to November no meetings were held due to insufficient trustees attending, then on November 7 the temporary bridge was ordered to be stopped up and the old houses taken down and materials sold. So even the trustees did not feel the event worthy of record.

Also noted was 'Early yesterday morning a gentleman of the city, out of great courage, and greater curiosity, ventured to ride over the New Bridge, but had not valour enough to return the same way.'; This local daredevil was George Catcott, a pewterer from south of the river, brother of Sandy the antiquarian [4], who 'gave the workmen a very handsome treat, to have the unspeakable honour to be the fist man that ever rode over the bridge. So exalted, like Mordecai the Jew on the horse Aha Sueris, he rode triumphantly over a few tottering planks his horse being guided by one of the labourers who acted the part of Haman in the great scene.'

When the spire of St Nicholas' church was completed in 1770, this same man placed the last stone on top, fixed with a brass plate to commemorate his act of bravery or recklessness. Latimer called him [5] "a bustling, but futile amateur in archaeology." He also had a large book collection, none of which was less than 100 years old, and his favourite author was Charles I, whose work he had mostly memorised. There really wasn't a lot to do in those days.

By July 1767 payment was made for all the arches being set, and a lighter was sunk trying to go through the wrong arch. By December the contractors had set twenty foot of cornice, then the following July the final payment was made, a total of

£9,300, a massive amount of money, so must have included stone and its quarrying and transport to the site.

Bridges claimed [6] that one of the reasons Edward's' bridges had fallen down was that he had used small stones, leaving too much of the arches made up of mortar, making them much weaker. Despite all the travelling done by Bridges in search of a suitable source of large blocks of stone, the contract went to the Courtfield Estate, owned by the Vaughan family, corporation bankers, far up the River Wye near Simmonds Yat. This site was a problem from the outset because when building was at its peak in summer, the river was at its lowest, making transport dangerous and unreliable.

Chamberlain's accounts note a single payment of £1,060 to the owner of Courtfield Estate in March 1762 [7]. Then ads were placed for other sources of the same stone, and masons and quarrymen were invited to contract for it. In 1766 the owner was paid the princely sum of £63 'as satisfaction for Inconveniences and Difficulties he has laboured under in consequence of his Bargemen not being properly Employ'd in bringing stone from his Quarry to Bristol for use of the bridge.'

Latimer claimed the bridge was opened to foot passengers in September 1768, on Michaelmas Day the Mayor was the first to traverse it in a carriage, and in November it was at last open to all traffic. But there is no record of any official opening or celebration.

By contrast, the opening of Westminster Bridge was widely advertised; the festivities were extravagant and prolonged: [8] On Saturday last a great Number of the Principal Inhabitants of the Parishes of St Margaret's and St John's Westminster met at the Bear at the Bridge Foot where, having dined, the following toasts were drunk, viz, The King with a discharge of 41 Pieces of Canon, accompanied with a flourish of Trumpets and Kettle Drums; the Prince and Princess of Wales with 31 ditto, the Pious memory of Queen Elizabeth with 41; the 42 members of the City & Liberty of Westminster and the rest of the Commissioners of the Bridge with 31. And having spent the Evening with much mirth and merry songs, particularly 2 new occasional ones with repeated Huzzas at ½ hour after 12 they march'd in Procession over the Bridge, proceeded by the Trumpets and Kettle Drums and saluted with 21 guns. On the Central Arch was played *God Save the King* and sung by all the Company; on their Return there was another Discharge of 21 Canon and the night was spent with the greatest Demonstrations of Joy that men sensible of so Public Benefit were capable of Expressing. The actual ceremony lasted 2 hours but for the rest of the day Westminster was like a fairground the river crowded with boats, the bridge packed with people passing to and fro and the pickpockets making a day of it with a roaring trade in purses and watches.'

Despite Farley's passionate support of the rebuilding, he is strangely silent on how and when it was opened. But he did publish an account of the unnamed mayor being the first to pass over the medieval structure, 'On Fridaie was the Time fixed for passing the newe Brydge About the Time of the Tollynge of the tenth Clock...' Another unnamed man wore 'a Girdle of Azure over his left shoulder, re- chde also to his Lends,' wherever that was. There were Minstrels and Claryons, and a 'Mickle Strong Manne in Armour' Saint Werburgh seems to have been popular at the time, along with Saints Kenya and Baldwin.

It reads like a load of old Baldwins, and so it proved to be -it was young Thomas Chatterton's first successful literary fraud. But it fooled many, including the brave pewterer George Catcott. He introduced the young clerk to antiquarian and surgeon William Barrett who gave him encouragement and access to his extensive library, allowing Thomas to seek greater heights of historical fantasy. It also triggered yet another round of arguments and pamphleteering in the city. And yet again, nobody came out of it with any credit. Catcott's passing over the bridge was ridiculed by Chatterton.

Materials of the temporary bridge were put up for auction in December, and again in May. The crane on Redcliffe side went under the hammer in December; that in St Nicholas not till the following May. A supervising mason fell off the top of one of the watch houses and broke his leg in July 1768, and in September the Gentlemen of Somerset met their President at the Exchange and crossed over the new bridge to a sermon at St Mary Redcliffe. The bridge's first fatality occurred in early February 1768 when the hard of hearing wife of farmer Tilley of Bedminster was run over by a cart when passing over the horseway of the bridge.

Bristol loved its public celebrations. Any victory in war, anniversaries such as His Majesty's birth or wedding day, or coronation, the birthday of local benefactor Colston, or the Gunpowder Plot were all celebrated with day long bell ringing, canons, bonfires, fireworks, drunks falling into the river and an occasional fatality.

Why was there no such celebration for the Bridge, so long demanded and so long argued over? Just more of this eerie silence.

Henry Bridges' Microcosm clock

Beyond the Bridge

When the bridge was completed and the materials of the temporary bridge and the cranes sold off, the main work of the Bridge Trustees was completed. They continued to hold their meetings on the first Monday of every month but as the years passed, they were increasingly deferred due to lack of attendance. This may have been the result of sheer exhaustion, or from the high mortality of the ageing Committee making it hard to summon the twenty plus required.

But there was still business to attend to. St Nicholas' church was rebuilt by Thomas Paty. The Trustees had allocated £1,400 towards this, but costs spiralled, the parish decided it wanted a larger church, and the wooden tower was found to be ruinous so needed rebuilding. A passage beside it was opened up for pedestrian access from the bridge to the markets. An Act of Parliament had to be taken out by the Vestry to raise funds, to which the Bridge Trustees contributed £1,000 of what, with the costs of the Act, eventually exceeded £7,000.

Avenues leading to the bridge needed rebuilding, so houses on the south side of the Shambles from Peter Street to St Nicholas' Gate were valued in December 1764[1]. Materials of the houses were sold off early the following year and houses purchased on adjoining Dolphin Lane. Early 1767 the mason Robert Gay had begun building the key wall behind The Shambles, which he completed late the following year for £1500, which must have covered labour, stone and shipping. He was then in charge of laying foundations for Bridge Street, earning him another thousand, along with various other tradesmen laying drains, paving the street etc.

The first sale of land on the new street was in June 1771 to Thomas Curtis Esq who paid £52, so it seemed the scheme was off to an impressive start, but the street that Trustees had hoped would pay off much of the debt attracted little interest. It probably didn't help that Clare Street, and again designed by Thomas Paty, was being build by private subscription at the same time. Properties there, between the Exchange and the new suburbs of Kingsdown and Clifton sold like hot cakes, whilst Bridge Street seemed more like stale bread.

Years later, residents were complaining to the Trustees about the state of the area, with many empty plots where filth was dumped, lowering values of adjoining properties and causing loss of trade. A fair enough complaint, but what could the Trustees have done about it? They specified high standards of buildings for the street, but many of those moving there had warehouses, and rather more down market properties. Having built half a street of fine 3 storey houses, should they have lowered their specifications to encourage the plots to be sold?

In 1779 the Trustees began developing Bath Street, which included amongst other properties, the Presbyterian Meeting House, in an old theatre which was once a gothic merchants house. It tells us much about early building techniques that they considered continuing in the building even after part of it was removed for the new street, but they eventually chose to be bought out and move to Bridge Street [2]. But whilst some locals welcomed the take-up of such a large plot, there was heated opposition from a local churchman who claimed there was a law against Non Conformists meeting so close to a parish church, that of St Mary le Port. This was of course proven to be nonsense. The church was entered from high ground, with entrances to several cellars below which they rented out to pay for their church, a clever plan later adopted by the General Hospital on Guinea St.

The original Bridge Act ran its course, but despite having paid off much of the debt, much still remained so another Act was applied for to allow the tolls to continue. This was opposed strenuously, amidst cries of fraud and mismanagement, especially about profits being made by those letting out the tolls. But it was framed by Thomas

Symons, Clerk to the Trustees and at a cost of over £800, made its way into law. The Chamberlain's Accounts read like an exhausted runner trying to make the finishing line. In the final decade or so the bridge debt was not very big, but payments such as £40 per year for the Clerk, 10 guineas for the accountant, plus interest and other charges drained away the dwindling incomes from tolls and others. Increasing opposition to the tolls meant the churchwardens had increasing problems collecting the bridge tax, so payments were often late and incomplete.

By 1793 it seemed the end was in sight. In the Trustees Minutes of April 1793, Messrs Harvey and Harvey said it would be practicable to payoff the outstanding £2,500 by 24 June 1794 so recommended notice to be placed in the papers to this effect. The Trustee's Broker announced there was enough money in hand to maintain the bridge, so the tolls would not be let beyond the next year. The Trustees did not deny this so the citizens were delighted. But in the midst of their celebration the Trustees advertised the tolls to be let another year. [3] 'Surprise sat on every countenance; whilst murmurs, and renewed calculations, were heard in every street.' Then some public spirited gents bought up the tolls for the remaining few days, the gates were thrown open and it was assumed the matter was ended. 'passengers went over the Bridge toll-free, for the first time, on the evening of Thursday, September 19th. A stranger would scarcely believe with what excessive gladness this act was accompanied on the part of the public: a gladness, which nothing but the idea of a deliverance from oppression could have excited. People of all descriptions lined the Bridge, and testified their approbation, whilst the populace huzzaed most vociferously, whenever a horse or carriage passed. Near the gates were a number of indiscreet persons, who, not content with being joyous spectators, thought proper to become actors upon this occasion; and having cut down the gates, which were the property of gentleman who had rented the tolls, they made a bonfire with then. This gave a fresh vigour to their joy, with which they were so madly intoxicated, as to pull down the tollboard.'

The Trustees responded by publishing extracts from the Act of Parliament which makes taking down the toll board punishable by death. But they failed to prove to the public that the Act was still in force, when many believed otherwise. Events escalated over the ensuing days, the militia were brought in, the Riot Act read several times and dozens of innocent bystanders killed or injured when the militia opened fire. The coroner's decision was wilful murder by persons unknown so nobody ever stood trial.

Thus the bridge debt was finally paid off. The building of Bristol Bridge had been inspired by scores of deaths, and the affair was finally ended by more bloodshed, the first riot Bristolians instead of the usual outsiders. In between were masses of petty squabbling, accusations of fraud and corruption. Nobody emerges from this with any credit. And it foreshadowed many of the problems Brunel later had in building the Clifton Suspension Bridge, as well as the more famous riots of 1831.

But the bridge still stands. The roadway widened an the arches obscured by Victorian columns, it is a strange hybrid. A building made of three ages, when Bristol's fortunes were on the rise.

Death and the Bridge

What, ultimately, went wrong here? How did a project so vital to the city's commerce and the welfare of its citizens manage to drag out for so many years? How could a plan to save lives end in slaughter of dozens of innocent people over 30 years later?

Qualification to become a Trustee was by inclination plus an annual income of £400 or estate worth £2000. Thus the men who put their names on the Act of 1760 were the great and good of the city, including the Mayor and Aldermen Dean and Prebendiaries of the Cathedral, Master, Wardens and Assistants of the Society of Merchants, Commissioners of Land Tax, Members of Parliament, Officers of the Guardians of the Poor. The 113 names [1] present a snapshot of Bristol society at the time, mostly merchants, but also bankers, apothecaries, attorneys, musicians and clerics. But there is no mention of local aristocrats. Sir John Phillips is the sole title holder. No Berkeleys or Beauforts, and only a single Smythe, and probably in the role of MP. The Innys family of Redland Court signed up, but the influential and numerous Elton dynasty were absent. Given that so many victims of the old bridge were poor, the presence of only two clerics seems abysmally low. There were some famous local surnames on the list, but they were all lesser relatives. A strangely lack-lustre line up.

After years of struggling to obtain a quorum for meetings, immediately following Bridges' departure, saw a massive 67 present to finally decide the plans of the bridge. For the first time, there were sightings of the Eltons, and Thomas Tyndal merchant banker. Wallis and many of the earlier trustees never again attended.

When investors were invited to raise funds to get the project started, it had to be repeatedly advertised, and those who eventually did sign up were again a rather forgettable lot. Despite the repeated reminders of the importance of the project, the cream of local society continued to avoid it like the plague.

In the aftermath of the Bridge Riots in 1793, pamphlets were published on what were the causes, most of which concerned financial mismanagement, and failure of the Trustees to disclose details. But the Corporation saw itself as an aristocracy, never disclosing details of its activities, so why should the Bridge Trustees have been any different?

But all this ignores the problem that was there at the beginning: the bridge project started out with no money.

The Corporation was not just the local government, it was a major public benefactor. It was solely responsible for the Lord Mayor's Chapel and the parish church of Temple, as well as donating to the repairs of other churches when required. It built the Exchange, St Nicholas and St James' markets, as well as laying out Union Street. When roads needed repairing, even well beyond the city limits, it often gave free gifts. When the wool producers of Chippenham wanted the navigation of the Avon to be extended from Bath to their town, they did not apply to the Corporation of Bath, the Las Vegas of its age, but to Bristol as it was in the latter's interest as home to so many wool merchants. It helped out widows and orphans, donated generously to hospitals and schools. They built a stone bridge at the head of the quay in 1766, ie at the height of the bridge affair for which, according to Mr Wallis, [2] they paid Mr Daniel £2,300.

They gave nothing towards the rebuilding of the bridge.

It was not even that they refused to pay -requests for money were sometimes ignored or refused. When Clare Street was being planned to connect Corn Street with the quay in the early 1770s the Corporation formed a committee to investigate it, but declined on the basis that they would not make money from it.

Giving money to rebuild the bridge was never publicly discussed by them.

The Merchant Venturers were also local benefactors, who ran a school for poor boys, and often matched donations from the Corporation for such matters as building The Exchange, rebuilding churches and the statue of King William on Queen Square.

They were never asked to contribute.

Robert Nugent or Lord Clare, long serving MP was a generous benefactor to the city. In one year of famine he hired a ship to import corn to feed the city's poor. When he was re-elected he gave £250 to the Corporation, which was entered into the Chamberlain's Accounts as a gift to the bridge rebuilding. But he never specified what his gift was to be used for; it was the Corporation's decision to allocate it to the bridge fund, so even the great Lord wasn't interested.

The only people who seemed to be reaching deep into their pockets were the executors of a wealthy widow, Mary Ann Peloquin, last of the city's wealthy Hugenot families who subscribed hundreds of pounds to the cause [3]. In her will she left thousands of pounds to local charities, and in 1766 when the Bridge Trustees decided to save money by reducing the interest being paid from four to three and a half percent, investors fled and her executors stepped into the breach -to the extraordinary amount of £10,000, so they saw it more as an act of charity than as a profitable investment, as in its original construction,

This lack of donations and investment caused the Trustees to borrow heavily, at a high rate of interest, siphoning off much needed funds from the outset. Loans on such high risk engineering work must have attracted high interest charges. Earlier in the century, the west had been beset by turnpike riots, so borrowing for toll roads was also seen as very high risk, thus making money harder to raise.

Whatever the reason for the lack of money, it seems not to have made it on record. It must have been common knowledge to all at the time, so obvious to al1 it didn't need to be written down.

What are we missing here?

Perhaps we are missing a large group of the population: [4] 'the poor not only escaped criticism, but also escaped notice... there were lists of charitable projects and foundations. Bristol was justly famous for its care of the socially deprived – John Howard the prison reformer, described the prisons in detail – crime being a particular province of the poor – but otherwise there was little mention of this aspect of life. Poverty and suffering were altogether too common in the 18th century to warrant special notice. Furthermore, the literate were writing about the literate for the literate.'

Westminster Bridge had been needed to connect the main port of London and Westminster to the growing southern parishes. As the city expanded, its need for importing food, especially for the poor in times of crisis, was a constant problem. Food in the southern parishes was 20% cheaper, as goods were sold at markets there before being transported across London Bridge. [5]

In Bristol, the situation was very different. The greater part of the city was north of the bridge, and the suburbs of Redland, Clifton and Cotham with their clean air and views became increasingly populated by the people who mattered. From the start of the century, anyone who could afford it was moving out of the centre. To halt the movement of money from central parishes, the Corporation and parishes tried to clean up the centre, to build wide streets full of fire safe houses. St Nicholas parish, which included half of Queen Square remained affluent, St Stephen's was also holding its own, with the other half of Queen Square plus Clare Street, lined with coffee houses, scientific instrument makers, and carver-gilders. But in the centre, old medieval houses remained and became home either to tenements or industries, especially metal works. This was not what the linen drapers, attorneys, brokers and peruke makers of the city wanted on their doorsteps.

Directly across the river was St Thomas's parish. In medieval times, it was a parish made rich by the wool trade, but had not recovered from its collapse. The run down area had become home to a new breed of person -the small industrialists, often newcomers to the city, often Nonconformists. A far cry from the fashionable, mostly Anglican, merchants on the northern bank of the river.

Daniel Shewring who initiated the project was from that. parish and he subsequently became active in property dealing and purchasing materials of old houses. As well as being compensated for his house on the bridge, he did very nicely out of the rebuilding, No less than eight feeoffees or trustees of the parish church became Bridge Trustees, a high proportion but perhaps understandable. In the old medieval city, rich and poor were neighbours, who took care of each other -not so much out of altruism, but because they had to. The new squares excluded trades and the poor, so mixing between classes was deliberately reduced. Thus the bridge affair points to a death of another kind -that of the old, medieval way of community life.

The medieval bridge was built to unite the two halves of the city. The 18th century tolls encouraged people and businesses to stay on their own side, so its effect was to further divide the city between the rich north and poor south, and to continue the decline in the southern parishes.

The sad fact is that if the bridge affair had been properly managed, it would have been built in a reasonable time by Bridges, a man of immense talent who could have changed the face of the city, if not the country, instead of fleeing to what seems to have been an early death in the colonies.

The project which should have been, as the Exchange before it, a source of civic pride and public benefit became an expensive, drawn out dispute. Had it received donations and proper funding from the outset, the debts would have been written off in a reasonable time and money could have been spent on cleaning up and rebuilding the old town centre.

The affair which began with the deaths of innocent pedestrians ended with yet more innocent deaths. Bristol's great and good showed themselves to be uninterested in the people they claimed to represent and foreshadows the more famous riot of 1831. Though much of the city remained medieval, even into the 20th century, this affair shows the people had become recognisably modern.

REFERENCES

The Bridge at the Place of the Bridge

BRO- Bristol Record Office, CBL Central Bristol Library, FFBJ Felix Farley's Bristol Journal,

(I) Lobel, M.D. and Carus-Wilson, E.M., 'Bristol' in M.D. Lobel (ed), *Atlas of Historic Towns. II.* London. 1975. p.7

(2) RJB Walker, *Old Westminster Bridge. The Bridge of Fools,* David and Charles, Newton Abbot, 1979 p 32

(3) *Adams' Chronicle of Bristol* J W Arrowsmith, Bristol 1910, p 21

(4) David Harrison, 'Bridges and the Local Historian' in *Local History Nov/Dec 2005* p 20

(4) ditto, p 20

(5) ditto,p 22

(6) ditto

(7) F. Neale, *William Worcestre: Topography of Medieval Bristol. Bristol Archeological Society* 2000

(8) The Great Red Book of Bristol , I October 1376

(9) John Latimer, The Annals of Bristol Vol I p 28

(10) Jeffries Collection Volume 12 p. 30 CBL

(11) John Latimer, the Annals of Bristol., Vol I P 52

(12) Adrian Tinniswood, *The Polite Tourist: A History of Country House Visiting.* National Trust London 1998, p. 5 I

(13) Jeffries Collection Volume 5 p. 142 CBL

(14) John Latimer, Annals of Bristol Vol I p. 33

(15) FFBJ, 17 June 1758, CBL

(16) Dragonwing -The London Bridge http://midtown.net/dragonwing/col9802.htm 23/11/2003

(17)Jonathan Schneer, *The Thames, England's River* Abacus, London, 2005 p 70

(18) FFBJ, 18 March 1758, CBL

(19) Bristol Corporation Chamberlain's Vouchers F/AC/Box 44/9, BRO

(20) FFBJ, II August 1759

(21) Notes taken from Exhibition 'London 1752', British Museum, 2003

(22) RJB Walker, *Old Westminster Bridge. The Bridge of Fools,* p. 48

(23) John Summerson, *Georgian London,* Pleiades Books, 1947 London, p. 10

(24) Patrick McGrath, ed. *Bristol in the Eighteenth Century* David & Charles, Newton Abbot, 1972, p.29

(25) FFBJ, 4 February 1758

(26) John Summerson, *Georgian London,* p. 96

(27) Do, p. 98

(28) Gwyndaf Breese, The Bridges of Wales, Gwasg Carreg Gwalch, Llanrwst, 2001

(29) RJB Walker, *Old Westminster Bridge. The Bridge of Fools,* p 221

Clearing the Jungle

(1) F. Neale, *William Worcestre: Topography of Medieval Bristol.*

(2) St Nicholas Parish Poor Rates. BRO

(3) St Thomas "   "

(4) The Act for Rebuilding Bristol Bridge, 1760, BCL

(5) Bristol bridge Chamberlain's Accounts BRO ref 09356

(6) Quarter Sessions Bridge Over Avon 1760-67 BRO Ref JQS/D/23

(7) Barrett, William. *The History and Antiquities of the City of Bristol.* Pub 1787 republished 1982. Alan Sutton Publishing Ltd, Gloucester p 97

Enacting the Act

(1)   Proceedings of the Common Council, BRO

(2) FFBJ 2 Feb 1760
(3) Letter Michael Miller to Jarrit Smith 31 Jan 1759, BRO Ref AC/C/II0/1-24
(4) Primary Sources of the Malago Society – Jarrit Smythe notes BRO ref 41648/P2/30
(5) Jeffries Collection Volume 5 p 142
(6) Bristol Bridge Act 1760

Building the Bridge

(1)   FFBJ, 8 November 1760
(2)   FFBJ 13 March 1762
(3) Barrett, William. *The History and* Antiquities *of the City of Bristol.* p. 97
(4) Minutes of Bridge Commissioners Meetings, 1- 93, CBL
(5) Roger Price, 'An Excavation at Bristol Bridge, Bristol 1975'
(6) FFBJ, 15 Aug 1760
(7) FFBJ, 18 February 1769
(8) Letter from John Wood to the Bridge Commissioners, Jeffries Collection Vol 8 p 30 CBL
(9) Chamberlain's Accounts for Bristol Bridge, July 1763, BRO Ref 09356(1)
(10) Minutes of Bridge Trustees
(11) FFBJ.II April 1761
(12) FFBJ 25 April 1761
(13) FFBJ 2 May 1761
(14)FFBJ 23 May 1761
(15) FFBJ 16 May 1761
(16) FFBJ *20* May 1769
(17) FFBJ 2 January 1762
(18) *An Intended Journey by Thomas Chrichlow and William Gorten April 24 1768,* Liverpool Record Office
(19) Jeffries Collection, Vol v p. 142
(20) FFBJ 16 July 1762
(21) Bridge Commissioners Minutes
(22) Chamberlain's Accounts for Bristol Bridge, BRO
(23) FFBJ 26 December 1761
(24) The Act for Rebuilding Bristol Bridge
(25)Chamberlain's Accounts for Bristol Bridge, 12 May 1768, BRO Ref 09356(1)
(26) FFBJ 29 May 1762
(27 Bridge Commissioners Minutes
(28) John Summerson, *Georgian London*, p 105
(29) FFBJ 19 February 1763
(30) FFBJ 12 March 1763
(31) FFBJ 26 March 1763
(32) Bridge Trustees Minutes
(33) FFBJ 13 August 1763
(34) FFBJ 29 October 1763
(35) FFBJ 5 November 1763
(36) FFBJ 19 November 1763
(37) FFBJ 10 December 1763

Gentlemen, & Players and a Giant Travelling Clock

(I) A Reply to a Most Partial Pamphlet, by A Citizen, CBL
(2) Mr Bridges' Further Observations on a New Stone Bridge, Jeffries Collection Vol, 8 p. 23
(3) FFBJ 29 May 1762
(4) H. Alan Lloyd, Some Outstanding Clocks over 700 years 1250-1950. Leonard Hill

Books, London 1958, p 95

(5) Millburn, John R, The Meandering Microcosm, in 'Antiquarian Horology and the Proceedings of the Antiquarian Horological Society', No. I, Vol 22, Spring 1995

(6) *Memoirs of R.L Edgeworth vol 1* Completed by J Marin, London, 1820, pp 110- III

(7) Henry Bridges. Last Will and Testament. Proven 3 July 1754. Public Record Office

(8) FFBJ January 1775

(9) Mr Wood's Reply, Jeffries Collection Vol 8 p. 29

(10) Bridge Trustees Minutes p 24

(11)Jeffries Collection vol 12 p 153 .

(12) Mr Wallis's answer to Mr Bridges' Pamphlet, Jeffries Collection Vol 8, p 124

(13) Ditto

(14) Jeffries Collection, vol 8 p.25

(15) Mr Wood's Reply, Jeffries Collection, vol 8 p29

Silent Opening

(I) RJB Walker, *Old Westminster Bridge, The Bridge of Fools,* p 95-6

(2) Chamberlain's Accounts for Bristol Bridge, BRO Ref 09356(1) (3) Bridge Trustees Minutes p. 33

(4) Jeffries Collection, vol 12, p. 315

(5) John Latimer, *The Annals of Bristol* Vol. 2, p. 383

(6) Jeffries Collection Volume 8 p.23

(7) Chamberlain's Accounts for Bristol Bridge, BRO Ref 09356(1)

(8) RJB Walker, *Old Westminster Bridge. The Bridge of Fools,*p.206

Beyond the Bridge

(1) Chamberlain's Accounts for Bristol Bridge,

(2) Bridge Street Chapel, BRO Ref 39399/CD/F/9

(1) *An Impartial History of the Late Disturbances in the City of Bristol.* CBL Ref L90.073

Death and the Bridge

(1)   Bristol Bridge Act 1760

(2)   Jeffries Collection vol 8 p 24

(3)   Chamberlain's Accounts for Bristol Bridge, BRO

(4)   Patrick McGrath, ed. *Bristol in the Eighteenth Century* David & Charles, Newton Abbot, 1972 p 38

(5)   RJB Walker, *Old Westminster Bridge, The Bridge of Fools.* p 48